Library of
Davidson College

Errors in Provisional Estimates
of Gross National Product

NATIONAL BUREAU OF ECONOMIC RESEARCH

Studies in Business Cycles

1. *Business Cycles: The Problem and Its Setting,* by Wesley C. Mitchell
2. *Measuring Business Cycles,* by Arthur F. Burns and Wesley C. Mitchell
3. *American Transportation in Prosperity and Depression,* by Thor Hultgren
4. *Inventories and Business Cycles, with Special Reference to Manufacturers' Inventories,* by Moses Abramovitz
5. *What Happens during Business Cycles: A Progress Report,* by Wesley C. Mitchell
6. *Personal Income during Business Cycles,* by Daniel Creamer with the assistance of Martin Bernstein
7. *Consumption and Business Fluctuations: A Case Study of the Shoe, Leather, Hide Sequence,* by Ruth P. Mack
8. *International Financial Transactions and Business Cycles,* by Oskar Morgenstern
9. *Federal Receipts and Expenditures During Business Cycles, 1879–1958,* by John M. Firestone
10. *Business Cycle Indicators:* Volume I, *Contributions to the Analysis of Current Business Conditions;* Volume II, *Basic Data on Cyclical Indicators;* edited by Geoffrey H. Moore
11. *Postwar Cycles in Manufacturers' Inventories,* by Thomas M. Stanback, Jr.
12. *A Monetary History of the United States, 1867–1960,* by Milton Friedman and Anna J. Schwartz
13. *Determinants and Effects of Changes in the Stock of Money, 1875–1960,* by Phillip Cagan
14. *Cost, Prices and Profits: Their Cyclical Relations,* by Thor Hultgren
15. *Cyclical Fluctuations in the Exports of the United States Since 1879,* by Ilse Mintz
16. *Information, Expectations, and Inventory Fluctuation: A Study of Materials Stock on Hand and on Order,* by Ruth P. Mack
17. *Forecasting and Recognizing Business Cycle Turning Points,* by Rendigs Fels and C. Elton Hinshaw
18. *The Business Cycle in a Changing World,* by Arthur F. Burns
19. *Economic Forecasts and Expectations,* by Jacob Mincer et al.
20. *Monetary Statistics of the United States: Estimates, Sources, Methods,* by Milton Friedman and Anna Jacobson Schwartz
21. *Errors in Provisional Estimates of Gross National Product,* by Rosanne Cole

ERRORS IN PROVISIONAL ESTIMATES OF GROSS NATIONAL PRODUCT

Rosanne Cole

National Bureau of Economic Research
NEW YORK   1969

DISTRIBUTED BY *Columbia University Press*
NEW YORK AND LONDON

339.3
C689e

Copyright © 1969 by the
National Bureau of Economic Research, Inc.
All rights reserved
L. C. CARD: 69-12463
SBN: 87014-207-0   74-1593
Printed in the United States of America

National Bureau of Economic Research

OFFICERS

Arthur F. Burns, *Honorary Chairman*
Theodore O. Yntema, *Chairman*
Walter W. Heller, *Vice Chairman*
John R. Meyer, *President*
Donald B. Woodward, *Treasurer*

Victor R. Fuchs, *Vice President-Research*
F. Thomas Juster, *Vice President-Research*
Douglas H. Eldridge, *Vice President-Administration*
Hal B. Lary, *Director of International Studies*

DIRECTORS AT LARGE

Joseph A. Beirne, *Communications Workers of America*
Arthur F. Burns, *Board of Governors of the Federal Reserve System*
Wallace J. Campbell, *Foundation for Cooperative Housing*
Erwin D. Canham, *Christian Science Monitor*
Robert A. Charpie, *The Cabot Corporation*
Solomon Fabricant, *New York University*
Frank W. Fetter, *Hanover, New Hampshire*
Eugene P. Foley, *Dreyfus Corporation*
Marion B. Folsom, *Rochester, New York*
Eli Goldston, *Eastern Gas and Fuel Associates*
Crawford H. Greenewalt, *E. I. du Pont de Nemours & Company*

David L. Grove, *IBM Corporation*
Walter W. Heller, *University of Minnesota*
Vivian W. Henderson, *Clark College*
John R. Meyer, *Yale University*
J. Irwin Miller, *Cummins Engine Company, Inc.*
Geoffrey H. Moore, *Bureau of Labor Statistics*
J. Wilson Newman, *Dun & Bradstreet, Inc.*
James J. O'Leary, *United States Trust Company of New York*
Robert V. Roosa, *Brown Brothers Harriman & Co.*
Boris Shishkin, *AFL-CIO*
Lazare Teper, *ILGWU*
Donald B. Woodward, *Riverside, Connecticut*
Theodore O. Yntema, *Oakland University*

DIRECTORS BY UNIVERSITY APPOINTMENT

Moses Abramovitz, *Stanford*
Gary S. Becker, *Columbia*
Charles H. Berry, *Princeton*
Francis M. Boddy, *Minnesota*
Tom E. Davis, *Cornell*
Otto Eckstein, *Harvard*
Walter D. Fisher, *Northwestern*
R. A. Gordon, *California*

Robert J. Lampman, *Wisconsin*
Maurice W. Lee, *North Carolina*
Lloyd G. Reynolds, *Yale*
Robert M. Solow, *Massachusetts Institute of Technology*
Henri Theil, *Chicago*
Thomas A. Wilson, *Toronto*
Willis J. Winn, *Pennsylvania*

DIRECTORS BY APPOINTMENT OF OTHER ORGANIZATIONS

Emilio G. Collado, *Committee for Economic Development*
Thomas D. Flynn, *American Institute of Certified Public Accountants*
Nathaniel Goldfinger, *AFL-CIO*
Harold G. Halcrow, *American Agricultural Economics Association*

Douglas G. Hartle, *Canadian Economics Association*
Walter E. Hoadley, *American Finance Association*
Douglass C. North, *Economic History Association*
Murray Shields, *American Management Association*
George Cline Smith, *National Association of Business Economists*
Willard L. Thorp, *American Economic Association*

W. Allen Wallis, *American Statistical Association*

DIRECTORS EMERITI

Percival F. Brundage
Gottfried Haberler

Albert J. Hettinger, Jr.
Harry W. Laidler

George B. Roberts
George Soule

Jacob Viner
Joseph H. Willits

SENIOR RESEARCH STAFF

Gary S. Becker
Phillip Cagan *
Alfred H. Conrad
James S. Earley
Solomon Fabricant
Milton Friedman
Victor R. Fuchs

Raymond W. Goldsmith
Jack M. Guttentag
Daniel M. Holland
F. Thomas Juster
C. Harry Kahn
John F. Kain
John W. Kendrick

Irving B. Kravis
Hal B. Lary
Robert E. Lipsey
John R. Meyer
Jacob Mincer
Ilse Mintz
Geoffrey H. Moore *

M. Ishaq Nadiri
Nancy Ruggles
Richard Ruggles
Robert P. Shay
George J. Stigler
Victor Zarnowitz

* On leave.

Relation of the Directors to the Work and Publications of the National Bureau of Economic Research

1. The object of the National Bureau of Economic Research is to ascertain and to present to the public important economic facts and their interpretation in a scientific and impartial manner. The Board of Directors is charged with the responsibility of ensuring that the work of the National Bureau is carried on in strict conformity with this object.

2. The President of the National Bureau shall submit to the Board of Directors, or to its Executive Committee, for their formal adoption all specific proposals for research to be instituted.

3. No research report shall be published until the President shall have submitted to each member of the Board the manuscript proposed for publication, and such information as will, in his opinion and in the opinion of the author, serve to determine the suitability of the report for publication in accordance with the principles of the National Bureau. Each manuscript shall contain a summary drawing attention to the nature and treatment of the problem studied, the character of the data and their utilization in the report, and the main conclusions reached.

4. For each manuscript so submitted, a special committee of the Board shall be appointed by majority agreement of the President and Vice Presidents (or by the Executive Committee in case of inability to decide on the part of the President and Vice Presidents), consisting of three directors selected as nearly as may be one from each general division of the Board. The names of the special manuscript committee shall be stated to each Director when the manuscript is submitted to him. It shall be the duty of each member of the special manuscript committee to read the manuscript. If each member of the manuscript committee signifies his approval within thirty days of the transmittal of the manuscript, the report may be published. If at the end of that period any member of the manuscript committee withholds his approval, the President shall then notify each member of the Board, requesting approval or disapproval of publication, and thirty days additional shall be granted for this purpose. The manuscript shall then not be published unless at least a majority of the entire Board who shall have voted on the proposal within the time fixed for the receipt of votes shall have approved.

5. No manuscript may be published, though approved by each member of the special manuscript committee, until forty-five days have elapsed from the transmittal of the report in manuscript form. The interval is allowed for the receipt of any memorandum of dissent or reservation, together with a brief statement of his reasons, that any member may wish to express; and such memorandum of dissent or reservation shall be published with the manuscript if he so desires. Publication does not, however, imply that each member of the Board has read the manuscript, or that either members of the Board in general or the special committee have passed on its validity in every detail.

6. Publications of the National Bureau issued for informational purposes concerning the work of the Bureau and its staff, or issued to inform the public of activities of Bureau staff, and volumes issued as a result of various conferences involving the National Bureau shall contain a specific disclaimer noting that such publication has not passed through the normal review procedures required in this resolution. The Executive Committee of the Board is charged with review of all such publications from time to time to ensure that they do not take on the character of formal research reports of the National Bureau, requiring formal Board approval.

7. Unless otherwise determined by the Board or exempted by the terms of paragraph 6, a copy of this resolution shall be printed in each National Bureau publication.

(Resolution adopted October 25, 1926 and revised February 6, 1933, February 24, 1941, and April 20, 1968)

Contents

Acknowledgments	xiii
Introduction	3
I. Errors in Estimates of GNP and Its Components	7
Data and Methods Used in GNP Estimation	8
Personal Consumption Expenditures: Commodities	9
Personal Consumption Expenditures: Services	10
New Construction	11
Producers' Durable Equipment	12
Change in Business Inventories	12
Net Exports of Goods and Services	13
Government Purchases of Goods and Services: Federal	13
Government Purchases of Goods and Services: State and Local	13
Types of Errors and Potential of the Revisions	14
II. Characteristics of the Revisions	16
Resemblance to Extrapolation Errors	17
Cyclical Characteristics	22
Overestimation, Underestimation, and Direction of Change Errors	23
III. Relative Accuracy of the Provisional Estimates	28
Provisional Estimates Compared with Forecasts	29
Provisional Estimates Compared with Extrapolations	35
IV. Gains in Accuracy from Additional Information	48
Gains Through Successive Revisions	48
Gains Over Time	56
V. Expenditures Estimates Compared with Income Estimates	62
Accuracy of Successive Estimates	62
Use of the Statistical Discrepancy to Measure Error	64

VI. Revisions in Major Patterns of Change   68

Cyclical Changes   68
    Amplitudes   69
    Turning-Point Dates   73
Revisions of Seasonal Factors   81
Postwar Trends   84
Comparison of Trend and Cyclical Errors   90

VII. Summary   91

Accuracy of the Provisional Estimates   92
Success of Revisions and Gains in Accuracy   93
Bias in the Initial Estimates of Change in GNP   94
Expenditures Compared to Income Estimates of GNP   95
Consequences for Users of Preliminary Data   96

Appendix: An Error Model   97

Errors in Provisional Estimates   101
Errors Measured by the Revisions   100

Index   104

Tables

1. Error Statistics for Provisional Estimates of Quarterly Levels and Changes in Gross National Product and Its Components, 1947 II–1961 IV — 20

2. Selected Error Statistics for Average Business Forecasts of Annual Levels of GNP and Its Major Components: Comparison of Errors Computed with Provisional and Revised Estimates of Actual Values, 1953–62 — 22

3. Mean Errors in Provisional Estimates of Quarterly Levels of GNP and Its Components Classified According to Cyclical Characteristics of Quarter Covered, 1947 II–1961 IV — 23

4. Types of Error in Provisional Estimates of Quarterly Change in Gross National and Its Components, 1947 II–1961 IV — 24

5. Errors in Successive Forecasts and Estimates of Annual Levels of Gross National Product and Its Major Components, 1953–62 — 31

6. Errors in Forecasts, Naive Model Projections, and Successive Estimates of Quarterly Levels of Gross National Product and Its Major Components, 1957 IV–1962 IV — 36

7. Errors in Naive Model Projections and Successive Estimates of Quarterly Levels and Changes in Gross National Product and Its Components, 1947 II–1961 IV — 41

8. Percentage of Error in Provisional Estimates of Quarterly Levels and Changes in Gross National Product and Its Components Eliminated in Each Successive Revision, 1947 II–1961 IV — 50

9. Coefficients of Correlation between Successive Revisions and Errors Eliminated in Subsequent Revisions of Estimates of Quarterly Levels and Changes in Gross National Product and Its Components, 1947 II–1961 IV — 52

10. Successive Revisions in Estimates of Quarterly Change in Gross National Product and Its Components Classified According to Success or Failure of Revisions — 53

Tables

11. Errors in Provisional Estimates of Quarterly Levels and Changes in Gross National Product and Its Components, 1947–54 Compared with 1955–61   57

12. Errors in Expenditures Estimates Compared with Errors in Income Estimates of Quarterly Levels and Changes in Gross National Product, 1947 II–1961 IV   63

13a. Revisions in Two Estimates of Peak to Trough Decline in GNP During Four Postwar Contractions, Classified by First to Latest Date Decline Measured   71

13b. Revisions in Two Estimates of Trough to Peak Increase in GNP During Three Postwar Expansions, Classified by First to Latest Date Increase Measured   72

14a. Revisions in Estimates of Peak to Trough Changes in Major Components of GNP During Four Postwar Contractions, Classified by First to Latest Date Contraction Measured   74

14b. Revisions in Estimates of Trough to Peak Changes in Major Components of GNP During Three Postwar Expansions, Classified by First to Latest Date Expansion Measured   76

15. Revisions in Major Turning Point Dates in Two Estimates of Gross National Product   78

16. First Compared with Revised Average Annual Rates of Increase in Two Estimates of GNP: 1947–63 and Subperiods   87

17. First Compared with Revised Average Annual Rates of Increase in Three Major GNP Components: 1947–55 and 1955–63   89

Charts

1. Root Mean Square Errors of Successive Forecasts and Estimates of Gross National Product and Its Major Components, Annual Levels, 1953–62   30

2. Root Mean Square Errors of Naive Projections, Forecasts, and Successive Estimates of Quarterly Levels in Gross National Product and Its Major Components, 1957 IV–1962 IV   34

3. Root Mean Square Errors of Naive Projections and Successive Estimates of Quarterly Levels and Changes in Gross National Product and Its Components, 1947 II–1961 IV   38

4. Errors in Provisional Estimates of Quarterly Levels of Gross National Product and Its Components, 1947 II–1961 IV   60

5. First and Revised Estimates of the Decline in GNP During Four Postwar Contractions and the First Year of Recovery   69

6. First and Revised Estimates of the Implicit Seasonal Factors for Gross National Product, Change in Business Inventories, and Total Final Purchases, 1947–63   83

Acknowledgments

This is one in a series of reports on the accuracy of short-term economic forecasting, a National Bureau project directed by Victor Zarnowitz. Financial support for the project has been provided by grants to the National Bureau from Whirlpool Corporation, General Electric Company, Ford Motor Company Fund, U.S. Steel Corporation, and the Relm Foundation, as well as by other funds of the National Bureau. A grant of electronic computer time to the National Bureau by the International Business Machines Corporation was used for some of the statistical analyses in this report.

Both Jacob Mincer and Victor Zarnowitz read and criticized the manuscript throughout its various stages. I am grateful for their encouragement, good advice, and important suggestions.

Geoffrey Moore, Julius Shiskin, and Phillip Cagan also provided many helpful suggestions. Stanley Diller, with whom I shared an office, was subjected almost daily to run-downs of problems and fine points, and gave help, richly laced with humor, on each one. Other members of the National Bureau staff, John Kendrick and Victor Fuchs, made useful comments on earlier versions of this report.

In the early stages of the study, I benefited from discussions with officials of several government agencies: George Jaszi of the Office of Business Economics and Milton Moss and Benjamin Teeter of the Office of Statistical Standards. In addition, Lawrence Grose of the OBE and Raymond Nassimbene of the OSS provided very helpful criticisms of the preliminary manuscript. I would also like to thank Francis M. Boddy, Gus Tyler and W. Allen Wallis of the National Bureau Directors' Reading Committee.

I am especially indebted to Johanna Stern under whose painstaking care the massive job of compiling the complete postwar record of gross national product estimates was done. Research assistants on the short-term forecasting project who helped with some of the statistical tabulations were Martha Callaghan Bergsten, Micaela Hickey, Dorothy Finger, and Cecilia Weidemann. The charts were expertly drawn by H. Irving Forman and the manuscript was edited by Gnomi Schrift Gouldin.

Errors in Provisional Estimates
of Gross National Product

Introduction

Gross national product has become one of the most widely used indicators of the nation's economic performance. Most evaluations of current business conditions and predictions of the future course of the economy rely in part on recent levels and changes in GNP. Movements in GNP are often used to assess the magnitude of short-term cyclical fluctuations and to measure secular trends in the economy's growth.

These uses of the product estimates require up-to-date and dependable figures. As so often the case with economic statistics, however, there is likely to be a trade-off between the accuracy and the currency of the estimates. An aggregate such as GNP is built up from detailed component estimates and much of the comprehensive data underlying the components is available only periodically or with reporting lags. As a result, the GNP estimates that are published on a current basis must be based on less comprehensive and complete data. These estimates are therefore provisional; they are periodically revised as more complete data become available. Typically, at least six estimates are made of the value of GNP for a given period.

This report explores the nature of the differences between the provisional and the revised estimates of GNP and its major components. Since the revised estimates are presumably more accurate, the differences (i.e., the revisions) may be considered a measure of the price, in terms of accuracy, of up-to-date GNP statistics.

A narrow view of GNP error is thus taken for the purpose of this study. The errors considered are measurement errors, given the particular definitions and scope of the present accounts. No attention is given to errors created by limitations of concepts, definitions, and coverage.[1]

Some of the sources of measurement errors and the potential of the revisions for reducing these errors are reviewed in Chapter I. Most ap-

---

[1] Recent work suggests that such errors may be large and that GNP in 1966 may have been understated by as much as 20 per cent. See Nancy and Richard Ruggles, *The Design of Economic Accounts,* New York, NBER, 1970.

praisals of the accuracy of the provisional estimates use the revisions as a measure of error.[2] No one, of course, in reviewing the record of revisions supposes that they measure the total error in the intitial estimates. Instead, they are generally thought to provide an indication of the uncertainty attached to the initial estimates, as well as a rough index of the reliability of the component estimates. For example, the studies by Jaszi and by Nassimbene and Teeter find some correspondence between the size of the revisions and the reliability that would be accorded the components by those most familiar with the estimating procedures and the underlying data: The GNP components which undergo the largest revisions turn out to be the ones considered least reliable, while the components which show the smallest revisions are considered most reliable. There are of course exceptions, and the fact that a component is not revised is no indication that it is more accurate than other components. It may simply mean that more reliable data have not become available.

On the other hand, the fact that a component is revised is no guarantee that it is more accurate. Indeed, one of the questions not explicitly considered in the earlier studies is whether or not the revisions actually improve the accuracy of the estimates. Though unlikely, it is nevertheless possible, as Morgenstern has emphasized, for the revisions to be perverse and augment measurement error.[3]

A direct answer to the question of whether the revised or the provisional figures are the more accurate would require estimates of the measurement errors in each set of figures—and it is well known that such estimates are exceedingly difficult to construct. As we shall see,

[2] For example, see Arnold Zellner, "A Statistical Analysis of Provisional Estimates of Gross National Product and Its Components, of Selected National Income Components, and of Personal Saving," *Journal of the American Statistical Association,* March 1958; Raymond Nassimbene and Benjamin T. Teeter, "Revisions of First Estimates of Quarter-to-Quarter Movement in Selected National Income Series, 1947–58," *Statistical Evaluation Reports, Report No. 2,* Office of Statistical Standards, Bureau of the Budget, Washington, D.C., 1960; Peter E. DeJanosi, "A Note on Provisional Estimates of the Gross National Product and Its Major Components," *Journal of Business,* October 1962; George Jaszi, "The Quarterly National Income and Product Accounts of the United States, 1942–62," in Simon Goldberg and Phyllis Deane, ed. *Studies in Short-Term National Accounts and Long-Term Economic Growth,* Income and Wealth: Series XI, London, 1965; and H. O. Stekler, "Data Revisions and Economic Forecasting," *Journal of the American Statistical Association,* June 1967.

[3] Oskar Morgenstern, *On the Accuracy of Economic Observations,* Princeton, 1963, pp. 261–272.

however, it is possible to infer at least the types of measurement errors that GNP may contain and some of the properties of these errors from the data and the methods used in GNP estimation. Even though this indirect approach does not yield estimates of the magnitude of the errors, it can nevertheless be used to show the rather special conditions that would have to obtain if the revisions were to augment error. The analysis in Chapter I concludes that in general the revisions could be expected to improve the accuracy of the estimates and, more specifically, to do so by eliminating extrapolation errors.

It is shown in Chapter II that the revisions are largest for those series which show considerable variability and weak serial correlation (i.e. correlation of an observation at one point in time with previous observations on the same series) and which would therefore be the most difficult to extrapolate accurately. Revisions therefore seem most common where extrapolation errors are most likely. Chapter III compares the magnitude of these "revision errors" with that of other forecast and extrapolation errors. Chapter IV considers how rapidly errors are reduced by revision and whether the accuracy of the provisional estimates has increased over the years. The results have some implications for the question of whether fewer revisions would suffice.

Earlier studies have given little attention to the whole sequence of estimates and revisions, or put differently, to the question of how rapidly the error in the initial estimates is reduced. Though Stekler's results suggest that the revisions after one month produce only a small reduction in error,[4] the effect of revisions thereafter has not been previously studied. Moreover, the earlier studies have not emphasized the similarities between provisional estimates and forecasts. The finding, however, that the revisions can be considered akin to extrapolation errors is relevant to the question of whether the provisional estimates have improved over the years. For example, Stekler found that the magnitude of the revisions has declined over time and concluded that the estimates have improved. Whether this apparent gain in accuracy occurred merely because the series were smoother in the later than in the early part of the postwar period and could therefore have been extrapolated more accurately is a question considered in Chapter IV.

Alternative estimates of GNP based on the income side of the ac-

[4] Stekler, *op. cit.*, Table 4 compared with Table 2.

counts can be derived (GNP, exclusive of the statistical discrepancy) and their accuracy is compared with that of the product, or expenditures, estimates in Chapter V. Following that, the revisions together with the statistical discrepancy are used to obtain very crude estimates of the error that may remain in GNP estimates.

The revisions of major patterns of change in GNP are reviewed in Chapter VI. It is generally, though mistakenly, supposed that the revisions mainly alter the level of the estimates and have little systematic effect on the changes. However, it is shown in Chapter VI that the initial estimates have tended to overestimate cyclical and underestimate trend movements in GNP throughout the postwar period. The cyclical errors were primarily the result of overestimating changes in gross private domestic investment; underestimating changes in personal consumption expenditures was the major source of the trend errors. During periods of business cycle contraction the two kinds of error reinforced each other and caused the initial estimates to exaggerate substantially the severity of peak to trough decline in GNP. The errors tend to offset one another during periods of expansion.

The revisions not only affected the amplitudes of cyclical changes; they also affected the dates of major turns. Peaks were not altered, but the dates of three of the four postwar lows in GNP were changed by a minimum of one quarter. Some evidence is presented that revisions in the seasonal factors were primarily responsible for the changes in turning point dates.

For the benefit of the impatient reader, the last chapter contains a fairly detailed summary of findings. The period covered by this report is the postwar years, 1947–63, although data compiled through the major revision of 1965 are used to appraise the earlier figures.

I

Errors in Estimates of GNP and Its Components

Gross national product estimates have been published on a current quarterly basis since 1947. They are built up from detailed component estimates. In the absence of a reporting system designed for GNP estimation, most of the data underlying the components are collected primarily for other purposes. The majority are government produced statistics and many are merely the by-product of administrative requirements. As a consequence, there is little opportunity for over-all quality control: The primary data differ in how up-to-date or frequently available they are and in how directly they measure components based on them.

The Office of Business Economics (OBE) of the Department of Commerce assembles the diverse and detailed information and from it constructs the national accounts estimates. The form of the accounts as we know them today was established in the major revision of 1947. At that time they were set more firmly into an accounting framework and separate estimates of both income and expenditures (product) accounts were constructed.

The statistical discrepancy is the item in the accounts which reconciles the income with the product estimates. Although the two estimates are not strictly independent inasmuch as some components of each rely on common data, they nevertheless provide the OBE with an important tool for controlling error. If a comparison reveals an unusually large discrepancy, it signals the presence of unusual error in one set of estimates or the other. An attempt is made to trace the source of error and eliminate it before the estimates are published.

Despite the usefulness of the discrepancy as a check on accuracy, measurement errors are of course present in the published statistics. The successive revisions of the estimates are designed to reduce these errors. To illustrate the types of error that the estimates may contain and the potential for reducing them, the section begins with a brief review of the data and methods used to construct GNP. Some of the sources of measurement error, the types of error that the revisions can be expected to eliminate, and some of the properties of these errors are then discussed.

Data and Methods Used in GNP Estimation

In the absence of a single body of comprehensive reports giving the income and expenditures accounts of consumer, producer, and government units, the national accounts estimates must be built up item-by-item from data obtained from a variety of sources.[5] Though the specific estimating procedures are exceedingly detailed and complex, estimation of the value of the majority of goods and services produced by the private sector of the economy consists essentially of two steps: (1) deriving benchmark estimates from detailed and comprehensive data for years in which such data are available; and (2) interpolating the estimates between and extrapolating them beyond benchmark years by means of related, continuous series.

The benchmark estimates for commodities are derived by the complex and rather roundabout "commodity flow method." This method, first developed by Simon Kuznets,[6] involves numerous estimating steps. First, the several thousand categories of commodities reported in the industrial censuses are classified as final or intermediate products, depending on the degree of processing and the use to which the goods are put. The final commodities are then allocated to either consumer or pro-

---

[5] A new publication is due shortly; at present, the sources for detailed descriptions are *National Income,* A Supplement to the *Survey of Current Business,* U.S. Dept. of Commerce (OBE), Washington, D.C., 1954, and *U.S. Income and Output,* A Supplement to the *Survey of Current Business,* U.S. Dept. of Commerce (OBE), Washington, D.C., 1958. For a short account, see Richard and Nancy D. Ruggles, *National Income Accounts and Income Analysis,* second edition, New York, 1956, Chapter 8.

[6] *Commodity Flow and Capital Formation,* New York, NBER, 1938.

ducers' durables catgories. The estimates must next be raised from producers' prices to final user expenditure levels by adding transportation costs, trade markups, and taxes. Finally, adjustments are made for exports, imports, and inventory changes. This laborious procedure of tracing the flow of commodities through each stage of the economic process —from production to wholesale and retail distribution to final purchasers—was adopted primarily because there were very detailed and comprehensive data available at the production level (the Census of Manufactures), but by comparison a small amount of such data at the wholesale and retail levels.

The data used to interpolate and extrapolate the benchmark estimates, other estimation methods, and the data underlying other GNP components are briefly described below.

PERSONAL CONSUMPTION EXPENDITURES: COMMODITIES. The Census of Manufactures is the main body of the data underlying benchmark estimates of consumer expenditures on goods. The estimates derived from these data by the commodity flow method have accounted for somewhat over 80 percent of consumer goods. Estimates of expenditures for other consumer goods (automobiles, gasoline, oil, other fuel, and tobacco products) are obtained by multiplying estimated quantities purchased by the appropriate average retail prices (the retail valuation method). The values of relatively minor items (food and fuel produced and consumed on farms and standard clothing issued to military personnel) are imputed.

The large body of retail sales data are principally used to interpolate the benchmark estimates between and to extrapolate them beyond census years, though some use is also made of state sales tax, federal excise tax, and trade association data. Retail sales by type of store are prepared by the Bureau of the Census from sample surveys. The data underlying the quarterly estimates are essentially the same as those used for annual estimates. The major difference is that advance sample returns are used for the provisional quarterly estimates.

Some shortcomings in the procedure of using retail sales to move the benchmark estimates from one census period to the next were revealed in the major revision of 1958. This revision incorporated new benchmarks derived from the 1954 Census of Manufactures. Comparison of the extrapolations for 1954 with the new benchmarks showed that, though the over-all totals agreed quite well, there were substantial differences among commodity groups. Tests based on the 1954 Census of Retail Trade indicated that the difficulty stemmed mainly from the use of retail sales data by type of store to estimate changes in consumer expenditures by commodity line.[7]

The practice of deriving secondary benchmarks from the Census Bureau's Annual Survey of Manufactures by an abbreviated commodity flow procedure was therefore instituted. These benchmarks, which are updated from year to year, are designed to help in spotting any biases that may be developing in the current extrapolations.

PERSONAL CONSUMPTION EXPENDITURES: SERVICES. No single body of comprehensive data such as that underlying the goods estimates is available for services. Estimates for the various categories of consumer services utilize a variety of heterogeneous sources. Estimates of the rental value of homes (nonfarm and farm) are benchmarked on the Census of Population and Housing and the Census of Agriculture. Expenditures for domestic service (cash payments and value of meals furnished) are based on wages paid. Outlays on household utilities are estimated from comprehensive annual reports of trade associations. Transportation expenditures are estimated from the annual report data of government agencies such as the Interstate Commerce Commission and the Federal Aviation Administration. Expenditures for professional services are benchmarked on sample information such as surveys of consumer expenditures, data from various professional associations and the Internal Revenue Service. Benchmark estimates for many other services such as auto and appliance maintenance and repairs, laundry, recreation, etc.

---

[7] Another difficulty arose when the estimates based on the new 1954 benchmark were fitted into the national accounts. The revised aggregate expenditures estimates considerably exceeded the income estimates, creating a large, positive statistical discrepancy throughout the 1948–54 period. It was decided to allocate the discrepancy rather than publish the revised estimates as they stood with their obvious shortcomings. Upon thorough review, it was concluded that the error could be attributed to the consumption estimates and they were accordingly reduced. A major factor in the decision was the fact that there is no body of data for the consumption estimates that is comparable to the highly reliable wage and salary component of the income estimates. In effect, consumption expenditures were estimated as a residual: personal disposable income less personal saving. (For a detailed account of the problem and its resolution, see *U.S. Income and Output,* Chapter 8, pp. 74–76).

are derived from the Census of Business. Other source data include the Census of Religious Bodies and the Biennial Survey of Education.

Though fairly reliable and comprehensive annual data for services are available from various government agencies and private sources, data for the quarterly estimates are much less satisfactory. Series used to interpolate and extrapolate estimates of the various service components are usually indirect measures of the particular component. Some extrapolations rely on estimated quantities multiplied by the revelant component of the BLS Consumer Price Index; others use payroll or employment data.

NEW CONSTRUCTION. Monthly series on new construction activity are prepared by the Bureau of the Census. Prior to 1959, they were prepared jointly by the Bureau of Labor Statistics and the Business and Defense Administration. Estimates of the construction component of business fixed investment—except farm and public utility construction and oil and gas well drilling—are principally derived from the monthly reports on contract awards issued by the F. W. Dodge Corporation. Data on building permits and reports on contract awards appearing in trade journals were used for geographical areas not covered by the Dodge series. Though the geographical coverage was expanded to the western states in 1956, the Dodge series must still be adjusted for undercoverage. Public utility construction is estimated from direct reports of work done or paid for from federal regulatory agencies, private corporations, and trade associations.

The 1950 benchmarks for nonfarm residential construction were developed from the 1950 BLS Survey of Consumer Expenditures and the Federal Reserve Board's Survey of Consumer Finances for 1951. Benchmark estimates are interpolated and extrapolated by series on building permits.

A difficulty in using the data on contract awards and building permits is that they must be adjusted to a work-put-in-place basis. This adjustment requires estimating (1) the varying time lags between the award of the contract and the start of work and (2) the variation in the rate of work progress after the start. Though the timing adjustments reduce the reliability of the annual estimates, the effects are even more serious for the quarterly estimates.

Comparisons of the housing statistics with information from the 1956

National Housing Inventory and the 1960 Census have revealed substantial underestimation of the number of dwelling units built in the postwar period. These findings led to large revisions in the estimates of residential construction activity by the Census Bureau after it assumed responsibility for compiling these series. The revised estimates were incorporated into the national accounts in the major revision of 1965.

PRODUCERS' DURABLE EQUIPMENT. Benchmark estimates of expenditures on producers' durable equipment are built up from the Census of Manufactures by the commodity flow method. Business passenger cars are the only sizeable component for which this method is not followed. Commodity flow estimates of producers' durables for other years are derived from the Census Bureau's Annual Survey of Manufactures, which was initiated in 1950.

The quarterly estimates are derived largely by interpolation and extrapolation of the annual estimates by an adjusted series based on the OBE-SEC Plant and Equipment Survey.[8] Since the quarterly figures on actual plant and equipment expenditures are not available in time for the provisional estimates, these estimates are based largely on the series of anticipated outlays.

CHANGE IN BUSINESS INVENTORIES. Tax return data compiled by the Internal Revenue Service and published in *Statistics of Income* are the basic source of information on business inventories. Returns for the corporate sector are available on an annual basis, but with a considerable publication lag.[9] Data for the noncorporate sector are available periodically from IRS and Census Bureau tabulations.

The reported data on business inventories require substantial adjustment to bring them to the national income concept of the change in inventories. Estimates are made, on an industry basis, of the portions of

---

[8] These data are collected in regular quarterly and annual surveys. They cover the whole of the private economy except for agriculture, professional practitioners, nonprofit institutions and finance, insurance, and real estate. The survey data are not directly incorporated into GNP because separate data are lacking for the noncovered sectors. Moreover, the survey does not provide a regular and comprehensive breakdown of expenditures into the separate categories of plant and equipment.

[9] Prior to 1958, the lag was about two and a half years. It was reduced by one year in 1958, when *Business Indicators,* a series of reports by IRS, was initiated. They contain advance information derived from samples of the data published later in complete form in *Statistics of Income.*

inventories that are reported on a LIFO and a nonLIFO basis. The nonLIFO inventories are then deflated by the revelant price components of the BLS wholesale price index and the change in the deflated beginning and year-end inventories is computed. This change is converted to current dollars to obtain the current value of the change in the volume of inventories. The adjustment procedure differs for inventories reported on a LIFO basis. Increases in LIFO inventories require no adjustment; decreases, however, require a conversion to current prices. Farm inventories are calculated by the Department of Agriculture according to the national income accounting concept.

Quarterly movements in the book value of inventories for manufacturing and trade are based on monthly sample data. Data for other components of nonfarm inventories are derived from the SEC quarterly reports on "working capital of United States corporations." These reports, however, are not available in time to be included in the provisional estimates. Farm inventories data are available only on an annual basis; quarterly estimates are obtained by fitting a smooth curve through the annual data.

NET EXPORTS OF GOODS AND SERVICES. These estimates are part of the regularly issued balance of payments reports. However, because of lags in source reporting, publication of the quarterly reports is not synchronized with GNP publication. The provisional estimates are therefore based on incomplete data.

GOVERNMENT PURCHASES OF GOODS AND SERVICES: FEDERAL. The basic sources of data are the annual Budget of the United States Government, the Daily Statement of the United States Treasury, and the Monthly Statement of Receipts and Expenditures of the United States Government. Some of the information used to convert these basic data to a national income accounting basis, however, is not available on a quarterly basis, or is not available in time for the provisional estimates.

GOVERNMENT PURCHASES OF GOODS AND SERVICES: STATE AND LOCAL. The major source of information is the summary statistics on state and local finances which are collected by the Bureau of the Census. These are essentially budgetary data and they require numerous adjustments to fit them into the framework of the national accounts.

The data underlying the quarterly estimates are reported payroll and construction outlays. Other categories of purchases are estimated on the basis of their past relationship to payrolls.

Types of Errors and Potential of the Revisions

Though the preceding sketch would hardly enable one to replicate the estimates, it is sufficient to illustrate that they are highly manufactured products. The resulting measurement error is therefore a conglomerate of errors whose magnitude is exceedingly difficult to determine.[10]

By way of contrast, it would be a fairly easy matter to assess the errors if GNP estimates were generated by a probability sampling process. For example, it would then be possible to attach confidence intervals to the estimates. Moreover, if the revisions represented a successive enlargement of a sample drawn from the same universe, there would be strong grounds for supposing that they improve accuracy.

Sampling error, however, is a fairly unimportant source of measurement errors in GNP. The major errors arise from the many gaps in the primary data. As we have seen, the comprehensive data underlying many GNP components are available only at infrequent intervals and long after the fact. These data are used to construct benchmark estimates. To provide continuous, up-to-date, quarterly series, the movements of related series are used to interpolate between the benchmarks and to extrapolate beyond them. There are then four major sources of error in the provisional estimates: (1) errors in the benchmark estimates; (2) measurement errors in the related series; (3) errors arising from an inexact or misspecified relationship between the two variables; and (4) errors arising from extrapolations of past benchmark values.[11]

---

[10] The only estimates of error that have been made are those by Simon Kuznets and they refer to his estimates of national income (*National Income and Its Composition, 1919–1938,* Volume II, New York, NBER, 1944). Under no illusion about the reliability of his error estimates, he states flatly that the task is an impossible one. ("Were we able to ascertain the sign and size of error for any given estimate, we could, of course, correct for this error and there would be no need to retain it," p. 535.) His error estimates were expert opinions, expressed in quantitative form.

[11] For a general discussion of the defects of widely used methods of interpolation and the advantages of a method which takes account of the correlation between the movements of the two series, see Milton Friedman, "The Interpolation of Time Series by Related Series," *Journal of the American Statistical Association,* December 1962, and reprinted as NBER Technical Paper 16.

The provisional estimates are revised as additional data become available. Minor revisions are made as a result of revisions in the related series. For example, the preliminary figures on retail sales are advance returns from sample surveys, and they are revised on the basis of more complete returns. Similarly, anticipated outlays on plant and equipment are replaced with realized outlays.

The availability of new Census data (Manufactures, Population and Housing, etc.) permits the construction of new benchmarks. Incorporation of the new benchmarks into the estimates constitutes a major revision: extrapolations of the last benchmark are replaced with interpolations between the last and the new benchmark.

The revisions could therefore be expected to improve the accuracy of GNP estimates in two ways: the minor revisions would be expected to reduce the component of error attributable to measurement errors in the related series; major revisions would eliminate the error due to extrapolating the last known benchmark.[12]

[12] It is often contended that the mere fact that GNP estimates are revised offers no guarantee that the revised estimates are more accurate than the initial figures. It is shown in Appendix I, however, that the errors in the provisional estimates would be expected to exceed the errors in the revised estimates provided that (1) the error in extrapolating the last benchmark exceeds the measurement errors in the new benchmark estimate; and (2) revisions of the related series reduce measurement errors in these series. Errors in the last benchmark estimate would be a component of the extrapolation error. Thus, in the absence of any evidence that the accuracy of the benchmark estimates and data for the related series have deteriorated over time, it seems reasonable to conclude that extrapolations of the last benchmarks are less accurate than interpolations between the last and new benchmarks and hence to reject the contention that the revised estimates are no more (let alone *less*) accurate than the provisional estimates.

II

Characteristics of the Revisions

The first estimates of GNP and its components in a given quarter are published one month following the close of the quarter. These are advance estimates prepared by the OBE for the Council of Economic Advisers for publication in *Economic Indicators* (*EI*) and in the *Economic Report of the President* (*ERP*). Revised but still provisional estimates are published one month later in the *Survey of Current Business* (*SCB*).[13] The provisional estimates are in turn revised in July of each of the following three years.

In addition to the three annual July revisions, the availability of new census data occasions a major benchmark revision. Such revisions have occurred in 1947, 1954, 1958, and more recently in 1965.

Incorporating new benchmarks into the estimates is a major undertaking and the opportunity is generally taken to supplement regularly used data with any new series that may have become available. For example, in the major revision of 1965, accuracy of the new 1958 benchmarks was increased by supplementing the census data with the improved data sources and estimating procedures used by the OBE to prepare the 1958 input-output table.[14] Changes in the 1958 benchmarks

---

[13] Provisional estimates have been published in *SCB* two months following the close of each quarter since the major revision of 1947. In 1950, the schedule was in effect moved up one month by publication of advance estimates in *EI*. In January 1963, the advance estimates were also published in *SCB* and they have been published there regularly since 1964.

[14] For example, in the report article on the 1965 major revisions ("The National Income and Product Accounts of the United States: Revised Estimates, 1929–64," *SCB*, August 1965), the OBE states (p. 7), "Construction of the input-output table required a complete accounting for all product flows—to industrial users of raw materials and semifinished products as well as to final markets. This provided a new and powerful cross-check, which improved the accuracy of the estimates of the level of GNP. In the prior bench mark revision, only sales to final markets

suggested by the input-output data led to a review and adjustment of the old 1947 and 1954 benchmarks and, as a consequence, a reworking of the income and product figures for the whole postwar period.

Major revisions have often involved definitional changes in addition to statistical revisions (that is, revisions which reduce statistical errors of measurement, given the particular concept, or definition, of GNP). The most important definitional changes were made in the major revision of 1947. Since then, the changes have been minor in the sense that none of the broad concepts underlying the accounts has been substantially altered.[15] The statistical revisions alone are relevant for appraising the accuracy of the early data, and it is generally possible to separate them from definitional changes.

There are then at least six estimates of the value of GNP for a given period. If A represents the true value of GNP, the advance estimates may be denoted by A_{00}. One month later, the provisional estimates (A_0) are published. The provisional estimates are in turn subject to three annual July revisions (A_1, A_2, and A_3, respectively), and, several years later, to one or more major benchmark revisions (A_n).

Resemblance to Extrapolation Errors

The provisional and benchmark revised estimates can be expressed as

$$A_0 = A + E_0 \text{ and } A_n = A + E_n,$$

the sum of the true value (A) and their respective measurement errors (E_0 and E_n). The cumulative revisions (ϵ) are defined as the difference between A_0 and A_n, which equals $E_0 - E_n$. Hopefully, the revisions measure the *reduction* in error in the provisional estimates though, strictly speaking, they measure merely the *change* in error from one set of estimates to another.

had been estimated, and no attempt made to ensure that—industry by industry—the implied sales of intermediate products to industrial users were consistent with information on purchases made by such users."

[15] There were some minor definitional changes in 1958 (e.g., cash grants to foreign countries were no longer added to federal government expenditures and deducted from exports of goods and services). Most notable of the changes in 1965 was in the treatment of interest paid by consumers; it is no longer considered part of total production, thereby lowering the estimates. See the report article on the 1965 revision "National Income and Product Accounts" *SCB,* August 1965, pp. 7–16, for an account of the definitional changes.

A simple error model is developed in the Appendix and used to illustrate some of the properties of the errors that would arise from the use of a related series to interpolate between two benchmark estimates; the errors that are introduced when the related series consists of preliminary data and is used to extrapolate the last benchmark; and the changes in errors when a new benchmark estimate is introduced. It is shown that the changes in errors (i.e., the revisions) would consist of two components: (1) the error in predicting the next benchmark estimate; and (2) the reduction in measurement error in the related series. The first component, the prediction error, would be a common element of the revision in each period and hence a source of positive serial correlation. It is next shown that if the prediction error were the most important component, then the revisions of the provisional estimates of the level would be larger than revisions of the estimates of the period-to-period change in A. Finally, if the benchmark predictions were extrapolations of the last known benchmark estimates, then the magnitude of the prediction error would be smaller, the smaller the variability and the greater the serial correlation in the series to be predicted.

If this error model provided an accurate description of the essential characteristics of the errors and revisions in the provisional estimates of GNP and its components,[16] then the revisions would be expected to have the following characteristics: First, if ϵ were primarily extrapolation error, the revisions would be larger, the greater the variability and the weaker the serial correlation in the benchmark period estimates. Moreover, revisions in the estimates of levels would be greater than revisions in the estimates of period-to-period changes; and finally, the revisions would be serially correlated.

Summary statistics of the revisions (ϵ) in the provisional estimates of quarterly levels and changes in GNP and its components are given in Table 1 (columns 2–4 and 7–9). The square root of some statistics (e.g., the standard deviation, rather than the variance) is used in order to keep them in the same units as GNP data (billions of dollars).

A comparison of the statistics for levels with the corresponding statistics for changes shows that the revisions in estimates of quarterly levels exceed those for changes for all except the two components estimated as residuals (change in business inventories and net exports).

---

[16] The model is clearly not applicable to the two components which are estimated as residuals (i.e., as the difference between two estimates): change in business inventories and net exports.

The table also shows the root mean square error ($\sqrt{M_X}$) of simple first order extrapolations (columns 5 and 10).[17] The statistic ($\sqrt{M_X}$) is computed as

$$(3) \qquad \sqrt{M_X} = (1 - r^2)S^2(A_n),$$

where r denotes the coefficient of serial correlation in A_n, the 1965 statistically revised data. The statistic $\sqrt{M_X}$ provides a rough index of the difficulty in extrapolating each of the variables given in Table 1. If the revisions resembled extrapolation errors, there would be a close correspondence between the ranks of $\sqrt{M_X}$ and $\sqrt{M_\epsilon}$.

Although there is a strong relation between the rankings of $\sqrt{M_\epsilon}$ for revisions of quarterly change estimates, there is almost none for levels (the Spearman coefficients of rank correlation are .89 and .27, respectively). The main reason for this discrepancy is the relatively large bias (mean error) in the early data for levels. A fairly strong association results if we ignore the level bias and compare the rankings of S_ϵ and $\sqrt{M_X}$ (the rank correlation coefficient is .77). Errors in the early data thus tend to be largest in those series which show the greatest variability and weakest serial correlation and which would therefore be the most difficult to extrapolate accurately.

The mean errors are negative for most of the variables in Table 1, suggesting that the provisional estimates tend to underestimate quarterly levels and changes. The degree of underestimation of changes, however, is negligible. With only the two exceptions noted earlier, the standard deviation of the error in levels exceeds that in changes. This result could occur only if there were strong positive serial correlation in the level errors.

The evidence in Table 1 is thus consistent with the hypothesis that the errors eliminated by the revisions are primarily extrapolation errors and that these errors are serially correlated.

One implication of the positive serial correlation in ϵ is that forecasts, to the extent that they rely on the provisional data available at the time

---

[17] If the extrapolation (X) were based on a first order autoregression,

$$A_t = \beta_0 + \beta_1 A_{t-1} + u_t,$$

where u_t is not correlated with A, not serially correlated, and has a mean value of zero, then the mean square error of X would equal

$$M_X = \sigma^2(u) = (1 - \rho^2)\sigma^2(A)$$

where ρ denotes the first order coefficient of serial correlation in A.

TABLE 1. Error Statistics for Provisional Estimates of Quarterly Levels and Changes in Gross National Product and Its Components, 1947 II–1961 IV[a]
(billion dollars)

			QUARTERLY LEVELS					QUARTERLY CHANGES			
		Average Level of Series	Mean Error	Standard Deviation of Error	Root Mean Square Error		Average Absolute Change	Mean Error	Standard Deviation of Error	Root Mean Square Error	
					Observed	Potential[b]				Observed	Potential[b]
Line	Variable	$\bar{A}_n$ (1)	$\bar{\epsilon}$ (2)	S_ϵ (3)	$\sqrt{M_\epsilon}$ (4)	$\sqrt{M_X}$ (5)	$\overline{|\Delta A_n|}$ (6)	$\bar{\epsilon}$ (7)	S_ϵ (8)	$\sqrt{M_\epsilon}$ (9)	$\sqrt{M_X}$ (10)
1	Gross National Product	382.7	−8.9	5.6	10.5	5.7	6.7	−0.6	3.2	3.2	5.3
2	Personal Consumption Expenditures	249.5	−4.4	3.3	5.5	3.0	3.7	−0.7	1.4	1.6	3.0
3	Durables	34.6	−2.6	1.8	3.2	1.9	1.4	−0.2	1.0	1.0	1.9
4	Nondurables	121.8	−3.3	2.3	4.0	1.4	1.4	−0.2	1.0	1.0	1.3
5	Services	93.1	−5.1	1.4	5.3	0.4	1.6	−0.3	0.7	0.8	0.7
6	Gross Private Domestic Investment	58.6	−3.4	3.5	4.9	4.6	4.0	0.0	2.7	2.7	4.6
7	Producers' durables	23.0	2.2	3.2	3.9	1.1	0.9	0.3	0.9	0.9	1.1
8	New construction	32.9	−4.8	2.8	5.5	1.1	0.9	−0.1	0.7	0.7	0.9
9	Change in business inventories	2.7	−0.8	2.7	2.8	3.6	3.0	−0.2	3.1	3.1	3.9
10	Gov't. Expenditures on Goods and Services	70.9	2.1	2.2	3.0	2.2	2.0	−0.1	1.3	1.3	1.7
11	Federal Government	41.2	2.0	2.2	3.0	2.2	1.6	−0.1	1.1	1.1	1.6
12	State and local governments	29.7	0.1	0.7	0.7	0.4	0.7	−0.0	0.4	0.4	0.4
13	Net Exports	3.7	−2.6	1.6	3.1	1.1	1.1	−0.1	1.7	1.7	1.1

[a]Errors are computed as $\epsilon = A_0 − A_n$, where A_0 stands for the 1965 statistically revised estimates and A_n, for the 1965 statistically revised estimates. The data are in current dollars, seasonally adjusted, at annual rates.

Provisional estimates are from issues of the *Survey of Current Business* two months following the close of the quarter covered. For example, provisional estimates of GNP's level during the 1948 II and its change from the first quarter to the second quarter are from the August 1948 *SCB*.

The 1965 statistically revised estimates are taken from the August 1965 *Survey of Current Business*. The figures published are the result of both statistical and definitional revisions. The major definitional change was to exclude interest paid by consumers from the estimates (see the report article on the 1965 revision, "National Income and Product Accounts," *SCB*, August 1965, Tables 2 and 3). This item was added to the published figures (expenditures on consumer services, and hence to the aggregates, personal consumption expenditures and gross national product) to obtain estimates of the statistically revised data. This procedure does not entirely eliminate the definitional changes and the resulting series (A_n) therefore includes some minor definitional changes.

[b]The potential root mean square error, $\sqrt{M_X}$, is computed as

$$\sqrt{M_X} = \sqrt{(1 − r^2) S_{A_n}^2}$$

where r is the coefficient of serial correlation in A_n. See text and footnote 17.

they are made, would predict A_0 more accurately than the final data, A_n. To illustrate, let P_t denote a forecast, made in period $t-1$, of the value of A in period t. P_t may be considered to consist partly of an extrapolative and partly of an "autonomous" component, as in

(3) $$P_t = \alpha_1 A_{0t-1} + \alpha_2 A_{0t-2} + \cdots + u_t,$$

where α denotes the weights assigned to past values of the series, and u an autonomous component which summarizes all other information on which the forecast may draw.

Any errors in past values of the series would thus be transmitted to the forecast and become a component of its error. This is seen by using the relation $A_0 = A_n + \epsilon$ to express P_t as

(3') $P_t = P'_t + \Sigma \alpha_j \epsilon_{t-j}$, where $P'_t = \alpha_1 A_{n_{t-1}} + \alpha_2 A_{n_{t-2}} + \cdots + u_t.$

The forecast error can be computed as

(4) $$E_{P_t} = P_t - A_{n_t} = (P'_t + \Sigma \alpha_j \epsilon_{t-j}) - A_{n_t},$$

or as

(5) $E^o_{P_t} = P_t - A_{o_t} = (P'_t + \Sigma \alpha_j \epsilon_{t-j}) - A_{n_t} - \epsilon_t = E_{P_t} - \epsilon_t.$

The variance of E^o_P equals

(6) $$\sigma^2(E^o_P) = \sigma^2(E_P) + \sigma^2(\epsilon) - 2r_{\epsilon E_P} \sigma(E_P) \sigma(\epsilon).$$

If the early data errors, ϵ, were merely random errors of measurement then ϵ would be unrelated to E_P (i.e., $r_{\epsilon E_P} = 0$ because ϵ would not be serially correlated) and the variance of E^o_P would exceed the variance of E_P. That is, the errors in forecasts measured as deviations from the provisional estimates would generally exceed the errors in forecasts measured from the revised estimates.

Table 2 shows statistics for the two measures of error in forecasts of annual levels of GNP and its major components. The forecasts are averages from Zarnowitz' sample of several hundred forecasts which were collected for the NBER short-term forecasting study.[18] They were issued during the fourth quarter of the base year and refer to the level of the variables during the coming year.

---

[18] For a description of the forecasts, see Victor Zarnowitz, *An Appraisal of Short-Term Economic Forecasts,* New York, NBER Occasional Paper 104, 1967, Chapter 1.

TABLE 2. Selected Error Statistics for Average Business Forecasts of Annual Levels of GNP and its Major Components: Comparison of Errors Computed with Provisional and Revised Estimates of Actual Values, 1953–62[a]
(billion dollars)

Line	Variable Forecast	Description of Error Measures[b]	Mean Error (1)	Standard Deviation of Error (2)	Mean Absolute Error (3)	Root Mean Square Error (4)
1	Gross National Product	$E°$	−5.4	9.3	9.0	10.3
2		E	−16.2	9.6	16.2	18.6
3	Personal Consumption Expenditures	$E°$	−1.8	4.3	3.5	4.5
4		E	−7.5	4.5	7.5	8.6
5	Gross Private Domestic Investment	$E°$	−1.4	5.3	4.7	5.2
6		E	−5.6	5.4	6.1	7.6
7	Gov't. Expenditures on Goods and Services	$E°$	0.7	1.8	1.7	1.9
8		E	1.6	2.8	2.4	3.1
9	Net Exports	$E°$	−0.3	1.6	1.2	1.5
10		E	−2.1	1.9	2.5	2.8

[a] Forecasts are from Zarnowitz' sample of short-term forecasts. See text and footnote 18.

[b] $E° = P - A_0$ and $E = P - A_n$, where P stands for forecast, A_0 for the provisional estimates, and A_n for the 1965 statistically revised estimates (see Table 1, note a for sources of data).

The forecasts and estimates refer to year T. P is published in the fourth quarter of year $T - 1$; A_0, in February of year $T + 1$.

Without exception, the error statistics based on E_P exceed those based on $E_P°$. The fact that S_E consistently exceeds $S_{E°}$ means that there is a strong positive correlation between ϵ and E_P. This correlation could be attributed to the forecasts' reliance on provisional data and the serial correlation of the errors in these data.

Cyclical Characteristics

Table 3 provides further evidence that the variability of errors in the provisional estimates of quarterly levels is not merely random. The error in an estimate of GNP level for a given quarter depends on that period's position in the business cycle. Provisional estimates tend to underestimate most during periods of expansion and underestimate less, or over-

TABLE 3. Mean Errors in Provisional Estimates of Quarterly Levels of GNP and Its Components Classified According to Cyclical Characteristics of Quarter Covered, 1947 II–1961 IV[a]
(billion dollars)

	MEAN ERROR OF ESTIMATES DURING:		
	Expansion		
Variable	First Year	Remainder	Contraction
Gross National Product	−5.5	−3.9	−2.5
Personal Consumption Expenditures	−2.9	−3.1	−2.3
Durables	−1.4	−1.9	−1.0
Nondurables	.1	1.7	.5
Services	−1.7	−3.0	−1.8
Gross Private Domestic Investment	−2.1	−.5	.4
Producers' durable equipment	.5	2.1	1.6
New construction	−.4	−2.0	−.6
Change in business inventories	−2.2	−.6	−.2
Gov't. Expenditures on Goods and Services	−.2	−.1	−.1
Federal government	.2	.2	.2
State and local governments	−.4	−.2	−.1
Net Exports of Goods and Services	−.3	−.2	−.5

NOTE: Details may not add to total because of rounding.

[a]Revisions after approximately three years (third July Revisions). Errors are computed as $A_0 - A_3$.

estimate, during periods of contraction. There is some suggestion that the initial figures underestimate more during the first year than in later periods of expansion.

The main source of underestimation is the personal consumption expenditures component. The cyclical differences are due mainly to errors in gross private domestic investment (especially in the inventories component), although there is also a slight tendency for the early consumption data to underestimate levels more during periods of business cycle expansion than during periods of contraction.

Overestimation, Underestimation, and Direction of Change Errors

Had the revisions merely changed the level of the estimates, they would have little or no systematic effect on the changes. Instead, as is shown in Table 4, the initial estimates of quarterly change in GNP tend to underestimate increases and overestimate decreases (lines 2 and 3).

TABLE 4. Types of Error in Provisional Estimates of Quarterly Change in Gross National Product and Its Components, 1947 II–1961 IV

Line	Type of Change in Revised Estimates (ΔA_n)	Total[b] (1)	Type of Error in Provisional Estimates (ΔA_0)[a]		
			Under-estimate[c] (2)	Over-estimate[d] (3)	Directional Error[e] (4)
		GROSS NATIONAL PRODUCT			
1	All observations	57	23	27	7
2	Increases	47	23	19	5
3	Decreases	10	0	8	2
		PERSONAL CONSUMPTION EXPENDITURES			
4	All observations	56	34	19	3
5	Increases	49	31	15	3
6	Decreases	7	3	4	0
		CONSUMER DURABLES			
7	All observations	54	16	31	7
8	Increases	33	13	14	6
9	Decreases	21	3	17	1
		CONSUMER NONDURABLES			
10	All observations	54	24	26	4
11	Increases	45	24	19	2
12	Decreases	9	0	7	2
		CONSUMER SERVICES			
13	All observations	55	41	13	1
14	Increases	54	41	13	0
15	Decreases	1	0	0	1
		GROSS PRIVATE DOMESTIC INVESTMENT			
16	All observations	58	26	24	8
17	Increases	37	17	15	5
18	Decreases	21	9	9	3
		PRODUCERS' DURABLE EQUIPMENT			
19	All observations	49	20	20	9
20	Increases	30	12	15	3
21	Decreases	19	8	5	6
		NEW CONSTRUCTION			
22	All observations	51	28	17	6
23	Increases	33	20	9	4
24	Decreases	18	8	8	2

Characteristics of the Revisions

TABLE 4. (concluded)

Line	Type of Change in Revised Estimates (ΔA_n)	Total[b] (1)	Type of Error in Provisional Estimates (ΔA_0)[a]		
			Under- estimate[c] (2)	Over- estimate[d] (3)	Directional Error[e] (4)
	CHANGE IN BUSINESS INVENTORIES				
25	All observations	57	18	27	12
26	Increases	30	10	13	7
27	Decreases	27	8	14	5
	GOV'T. EXPENDITURES ON GOODS AND SERVICES				
28	All observations	57	26	23	8
29	Increases	45	23	18	4
30	Decreases	12	3	5	4
	FEDERAL GOVERNMENT				
31	All observations	58	19	29	10
32	Increases	37	12	18	7
33	Decreases	21	7	11	3
	STATE AND LOCAL GOVERNMENTS				
34	All observations	52	25	23	4
35	Increases	51	25	23	3
36	Decreases	1	0	0	1
	NET EXPORTS				
37	All observations	56	26	22	8
38	Increases	30	10	15	5
39	Decreases	26	16	7	3

[a]See TABLE 1 note a and TABLE 7 note b for a description of the changes used.
[b]Maximum number of observations is 59. Cases in which the quarterly change, ΔA_n, is zero and in which $\Delta A_0 = \Delta A_n$ are excluded.
[c]Provisional estimate is less than revised estimate ($\Delta A_0 < \Delta A_n$).
[d]Provisional estimate exceeds revised estimate ($\Delta A_0 > \Delta A_n$).
[e]Sign $\Delta A_0 \neq$ sign ΔA_n.

Failure to distinguish between increases and decreases gives a considerably different impression of the error characteristics. It would appear there is a slight tendency to overestimate when all changes in GNP are considered (line 1). However, this is due mainly to overestimation of the relatively few decreases that occurred (compare lines 1, 2, and 3).

Most of the underestimation of increases in the aggregate comes from underestimating increases in consumption expenditures, particularly services, while decreases in consumer goods, business inventories, and federal government expenditures are initially overstated. In fact, the early figures on inventories and federal government expenditures tend to overstate both increases and decreases.

One could expect that the systematic errors in the early GNP statistics would be transferred to forecasts, which may consist partly of extrapolations of these data.[19] In fact, Zarnowitz, in his evaluation of forecasting accuracy, does find errors of a somewhat similar nature.[20] The forecasts in his sample tend to underestimate levels, particularly of GNP and personal consumption expenditures. Furthermore, the magnitude of error in forecasts, just as in the early GNP data, varies according to the stage of the business cycle. The forecasts underestimate GNP levels most during the first year of expansion. GNP levels during the remaining periods of expansion are underestimated by a lesser amount and they tend to be slightly overestimated during periods of contraction.

While forecasts of annual change tend to overestimate as often as underestimate changes in gross private domestic investment (both increases and decreases), increases in GNP and consumption are underestimated. There was no indication of bias, however, in forecasts of decreases in GNP.

Directional errors were much more frequent for series that have a more nearly equal distribution of increases and decreases than for series that show a great preponderance of increases (Table 4). For example, this type of error accounted for only 5 per cent of the errors in total consumption expenditures as compared with 14 per cent for gross private domestic investment, or 2 per cent for consumer services as compared with 21 per cent for business inventory change.

In contrast to the relatively few directional errors in the provisional data (12.2 per cent), Zarnowitz finds that forecasts show a very poor record in predicting the direction of the next quarter's GNP movement. This type of error ranged from 23 to 44 per cent in three of the fore-

---

[19] A detailed analysis of the effects of data errors on forecasting accuracy is given in R. Cole, "Data Errors and Forecasting Accuracy," in Jacob Mincer, ed., *Economic Forecasts and Expectations: Analyses of Forecasting Behavior and Performance,* New York, NBER, 1969, pp. 47–82.

[20] Zarnowitz, *An Appraisal of Short-Term Economic Forecasts,* Tables 3, 7, and 11.

cast sets that he examined.[21] In addition, he found that major turning points are often missed while false turns are occasionally predicted. Most frequently missed by the forecasts were the declines in GNP.

In summary, we can conclude that: (1) the revisions of the provisional estimates can be considered primarily a measure of extrapolation errors and (2) these errors are by no means random. There are systematic differences between the first and revised estimates of quarter-to-quarter change in GNP and many of its components, as well as between the estimates of quarterly levels. The provisional estimates underestimate GNP levels most during the early periods (the first year) of business cycle expansion, somewhat less throughout later periods of expansion, and still less during periods of contraction. Moreover, these characteristics of errors in the early GNP data are similar to those Zarnowitz found in his sample of forecasts.

[21] *Ibid.,* Table 13.

III

Relative Accuracy of the Provisional Estimates

It was shown in the last Chapter that the revisions can be considered, at least in part, to be a measure of extrapolation error in the provisional estimates. This result suggests that the accuracy of other forecasts (or extrapolations) would be a relevant standard, or yardstick, by which to assess the accuracy of the provisional estimates.

The body of information on which forecasts draw is also available for use in preparing the advance and provisional estimates. This information falls roughly into two classes: data currently available but referring to the future, such as anticipations series, and data referring to the past. The latter set includes past values of the variable to be predicted and historical relationships between this variable and others. Such relationships may be suggested by theoretical considerations, or they may merely summarize a tendency for movements in a particular variable or combination of variables to lead and hence anticipate movements in the target variable. Forecasts may consist of only a combination of past values of the series (as do naive and autoregressive model projections) or they may rely on historical relationships with other variables.

The job of the forecaster, just as of the data compiler, is to combine all of the relevent information at hand into an accurate prediction of the true value, A, such that the sequence of forecasts (P), advance (A_{00}), provisional (A_0), and revised estimates (A_j) is a sequence of predictions each more accurate than the last. A minimum requirement, then, for the accuracy of the official estimates is that they should be more accurate than the best forecasts of A.

Provisional Estimates Compared with Forecasts

Chart 1 shows the root mean square errors of a sequence of forecasts and estimates of annual levels of GNP and its major components covering the period 1953–62. The forecasts are averages from Zarnowitz' sample of several hundred forecasts.[22]

In the case of GNP, forecasts (P_1) of the annual level in year T are made in July of year $T - 1$ and revised in December (P_2). Further revisions take place in July (P_3) and December (P_4) of year T. Strictly considered, P_3 and P_4 are no longer bona fide forecasts inasmuch as they contain information from year T. Provisional estimates of the value of GNP in the first quarter of year T are available for use in P_3 so only the last three quarters need to be forecast. Similarly, P_4 contains a forecast only of the fourth quarter. Advance estimates (A_{00}) are published in January and provisional estimates (A_0) in February of year $T + 1$. The estimates are further revised in July of years $T + 1$, $T + 2$, and $T + 3$ (A_1, A_2, and A_3 respectively.)

Zarnowitz' sample contains no forecasts of the major GNP components made at the same time as the GNP forecasts P_1 and P_3. The first component forecasts (denoted as P_2 only to indicate that they were prepared at the same time as the GNP forecasts P_2) were made in December of year $T - 1$ and revised one year later (P_4).

Chart 1 not surprisingly shows that on the average the business forecasts are considerably less accurate than the official estimates of annual levels in GNP and its major components during the period 1953–62. But the chart also shows the advance (A_{00}) and provisional estimates (A_0) to be only about as accurate or, in some cases, slightly less accurate than forecasters' estimates of current levels (P_4).

Table 5 gives error statistics for the forecasts and estimates shown in Chart 1. The mean errors for GNP and three of its four major components are negative, indicating that the forecasts as well as the official

---

[22] There are no official forecasts of GNP in the sense that no government agency publishes a series of GNP anticipations. Since the early sixties, however, forecasts of GNP for the coming year, prepared by the Council of Economic Advisers, have been published in the *Economic Report of the President*. These forecasts might be considered official, but their record is too short for use here.

CHART 1. Root Mean Square Errors of Successive Forecasts (P_j) and Estimates (A_j) of Gross National Product and Its Components, Annual Levels, 1953–62 [a]

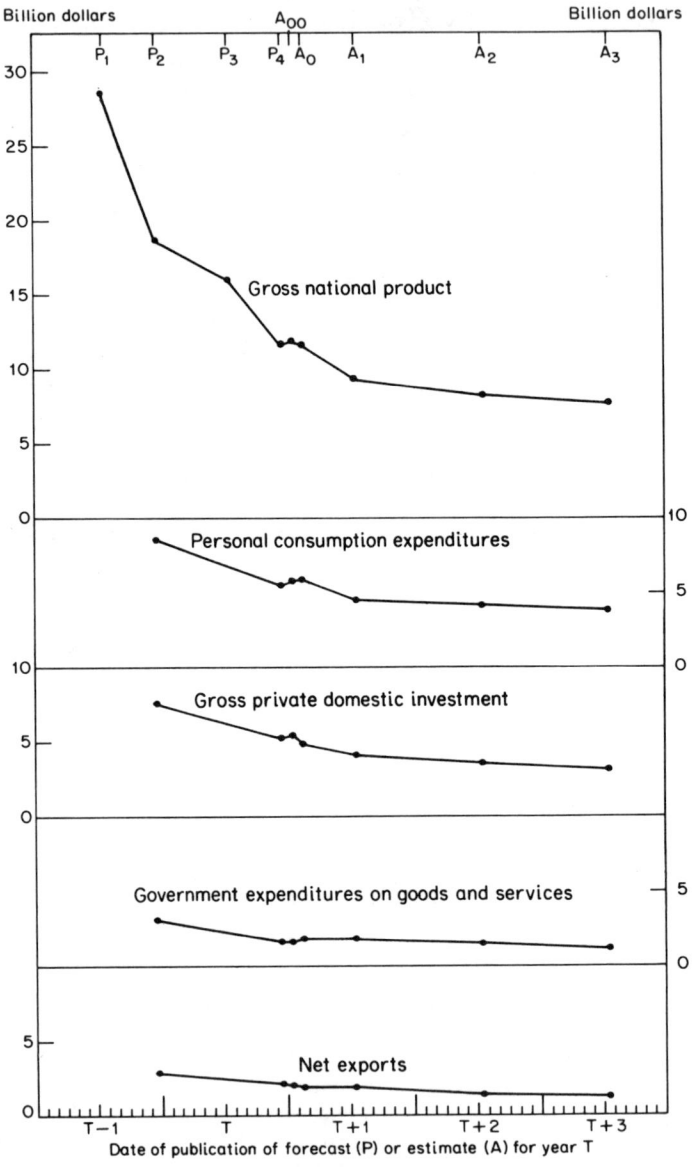

[a] See Table 5, note a, for a description of the forecasts and estimates.

TABLE 5. Errors in Successive Forecasts and Estimates of Annual Levels of Gross National Product and Its Major Components, 1953–62[a]

Line	Code of Forecasts and Estimates of Value of Variable in Year T[b]	Time Forecast or Estimate For Year T Published	Mean Error (1)	Standard Deviation of Error (billion dollars) (2)	Mean Absolute Error (3)	Root Mean Square Error (4)
		GROSS NATIONAL PRODUCT				
1	P_1: Average business forecast	July, $T-1$	−23.7	16.9	23.7	28.6
2	P_2: Revised forecast	Oct.–Dec., $T-1$	−16.2	9.6	16.2	18.6
3	P_3: Revised forecast	July, T	−14.0	8.2	14.0	16.0
4	P_4: Revised forecast	Oct.–Dec., T	−10.6	5.1	10.7	11.6
5	A_{00}: Advance estimates	Jan., $T+1$	−11.0	4.6	11.0	11.9
6	A_0: Provisional estimates	Feb., $T+1$	−10.8	4.5	10.8	11.6
7	A_1: First July revised estimates	July, $T+1$	−8.9	3.0	8.9	9.3
8	A_2: Second July revised estimates	July, $T+2$	−7.8	2.7	7.8	8.3
9	A_3: Third July revised estimates	July, $T+3$	−7.3	2.4	7.3	7.7
		PERSONAL CONSUMPTION EXPENDITURES				
10	P_2	Dec., $T-1$	−7.5	4.5	7.5	8.6
11	P_4	Dec., T	−4.4	3.4	5.3	5.5
12	A_{00}	Jan., $T+1$	−5.6	1.2	5.6	5.7
13	A_0	Feb., $T+1$	−5.7	1.1	5.7	5.8
14	A_1	July, $T+1$	−4.3	1.4	4.3	4.5
15	A_2	July, $T+2$	−4.0	1.4	4.0	4.2
16	A_3	July, $T+3$	−3.7	1.5	3.7	3.9
		GROSS PRIVATE DOMESTIC INVESTMENT				
17	P_2	Dec., $T-1$	−5.6	5.4	6.1	7.6
18	P_4	Dec., T	−4.4	3.0	4.6	5.3
19	A_{00}	Jan., $T+1$	−4.3	3.2	4.9	5.3
20	A_0	Feb., $T+1$	−4.1	2.8	4.4	4.9
21	A_1	July, $T+1$	−3.7	1.7	3.7	4.1
22	A_2	July, $T+2$	−3.2	1.7	3.2	3.6
23	A_3	July, $T+3$	−3.0	0.8	3.0	3.1
		GOV'T. EXPENDITURES ON GOODS AND SERVICES				
24	P_2	Dec., $T-1$	1.6	2.8	2.4	3.1
25	P_4	Dec., T	0.9	1.3	1.3	1.6
26	A_{00}	Jan., $T+1$	0.7	1.5	1.3	1.6
27	A_0	Feb., $T+1$	0.8	1.7	1.4	1.8
28	A_1	July, $T+1$	1.0	1.5	1.4	1.8
29	A_2	July, $T+2$	0.8	1.4	1.1	1.5
30	A_3	July, $T+3$	0.6	1.1	.9	1.2

TABLE 5. Errors in Successive Forecasts and Estimates of Annual Levels of Gross National Product and Its Major Components, 1953–62[a] (concluded)

Line	Code of Forecasts and Estimates of Value of Variable in Year T[b]	Time Forecast or Estimate For Year T Published	Mean Error (1)	Standard Deviation of Error (billion dollars) (2)	Mean Absolute Error (3)	Root Mean Square Error (4)
			NET EXPORTS			
31	P_2	Dec., $T-1$	−2.1	1.9	2.5	2.8
32	P_4	Dec., T	−1.8	1.0	1.8	2.1
33	A_{00}	Jan., $T+1$	−1.9	0.6	1.9	2.0
34	A_0	Feb., $T+1$	−1.8	0.7	1.8	1.9
35	A_1	July, $T+1$	−1.8	0.6	1.8	1.9
36	A_2	July, $T+2$	−1.0	1.1	1.4	1.4
37	A_3	July, $T+3$	−0.8	0.9	1.2	1.2

[a] Forecasts and estimates are of current dollar GNP and components. Errors are computed as $E_j = P_j - A_n$ for forecasts and $\epsilon_j = A_j - A_n$ for the official estimates.

[b] The forecasts are from Zarnowitz' sample of business forecasts (see note 21 in text). The GNP forecasts P_2 and P_4 are averages based on the eight sets of forecasts, coded A through H and described in his Occasional Paper *Appraisal of Short-Term Forecasts*, Chapter 1, as well as a ninth set which was not available in time to be included in his paper. P_1 and P_3 are averages of two sets (G and the new set, coded I). The component forecasts are averages of two sets (B and F).

The advance estimates (A_{00}) are taken from the *Economic Report of the President*. The provisional estimates (A_0) are published in the *Survey of Current Business* in February of the following year. For example, provisional estimates of the values of GNP and its components in 1954 are from the February 1955 issue of *SCB*. The first July revised estimates (A_1) are published in the following July issue of *SCB* (in the example, July 1955). Further annual July revisions (A_2 and A_3) are published in July issues of *SCB* for the next two years (July 1956 and 1957).

The 1965 major revision of the estimates is from the report article in the August 1965 *SCB*. The figures published are the result of both statistical and definitional revisions. The major definitional change was to exclude interest paid by consumers from the estimates (see the preliminary report article, "National Income and Product Estimates," Tables 2 and 3). This item is added to the published figures to obtain estimates of the statistically revised figures. The procedure does not entirely eliminate the definitional changes so the resulting series (A_n) includes some minor definitional revisions.

estimates underestimated the annual levels of these variables. Government expenditures on goods and services were overestimated on the average.[23]

[23] As noted in footnote b of Table 5, definitional changes have not been entirely eliminated from the 1965 data. Consequently, the forecast and data errors reflect in addition to statistical error some minor definitional changes.

The 1965 definitional changes tended to lower the official estimates while the statistical revisions tend to raise them. As an average for the years 1953, 1957, 1958, and 1960, definitional changes lowered the figures for GNP by $6.5 billions; personal consumption expenditures by $6.6 billions; gross private domestic investment by $.4 billion; and government expenditures on goods and services by $.3 billion. The estimates of net exports were raised by $.9 billion. (See the preli-

Even though they are slightly more efficient, the advance (A_{00}) and provisional estimates (A_0) are also slightly more biased than forecasters' estimates of the current levels (P_4) of GNP, personal consumption expenditures, and net exports. The opposite is true of the errors in gross private domestic investment and government expenditures; P_4 is slightly more efficient, but also more biased than A_{00} and A_0.

Although the differences in accuracy are small, the results are nevertheless surprising. One might have expected A_{00} and A_0 to be consistently more accurate (i.e., less biased and more efficient) than P_4.[24]

The only differences among A_{00}, A_0, and P_4 occur in the estimates of the fourth quarter of year T. In other words, all three are averages of the values of the target variable in the four quarters of the year and the same figures for the first three quarters are used in each. Thus any differences in the accuracy of the three sets of annual estimates arise from errors in estimating the fourth quarter.

However, the accuracy of P_4 is by no means an indication of typical forecasting accuracy. P_4 is constructed as an average of many forecasters' estimates and, because of the possibility of offsetting errors, it may be considerably more accurate than typical forecasts. P_4 might therefore be considered an unreasonably high, or unfair, standard of accuracy. For this reason, the quarterly data will be compared with a "typical" forecast.[25]

When all four quarters of the year are considered, the advance and provisional estimates compare very favorably with a *typical* forecast. The

minary report article on the 1965 major revision, "National Income and Product Account", *SCB,* August 1965, Table 2.)

It was noted earlier that the major definitional change was to exclude interest paid by consumers from the product estimates. This item averaged $5.7 billions for the years just mentioned. It was added to the estimates to obtain the series of 1965 statistically revised data. Somewhat under 15 per cent of the definitional changes, therefore, remain in the data used as "final" estimates.

[24] Other results are also contrary to this expectation. H. Theil finds over the same period, 1953–62, that the estimates of current annual changes in roughly half of the variables included in the Dutch official forecasts are more accurate than the Central Bureau of Statistics first (preliminary) figures (*Applied Economic Forecasting,* Chicago, 1966, pp. 140–150).

[25] Only one set of forecasts (Set C) in Zarnowitz' sample contains forecasts of GNP and its major components in quarterly units. The period covered by Chart 2 and Table 6 is therefore limited to the period for which these forecasts are available, 1957 IV–1962 IV. Comparisons of this set's annual forecasts with those of other sets justify its classification as "typical" (see Zarnowitz, *Appraisal of Short-Term Forecasts,* Chapter 7).

CHART 2. Root Mean Square Errors of Naive Projections (N), Forecasts (P), and Successive Estimates (A_j) of Quarterly Levels in Gross National Product and Its Major Components, 1957 IV–1962 IV [a]

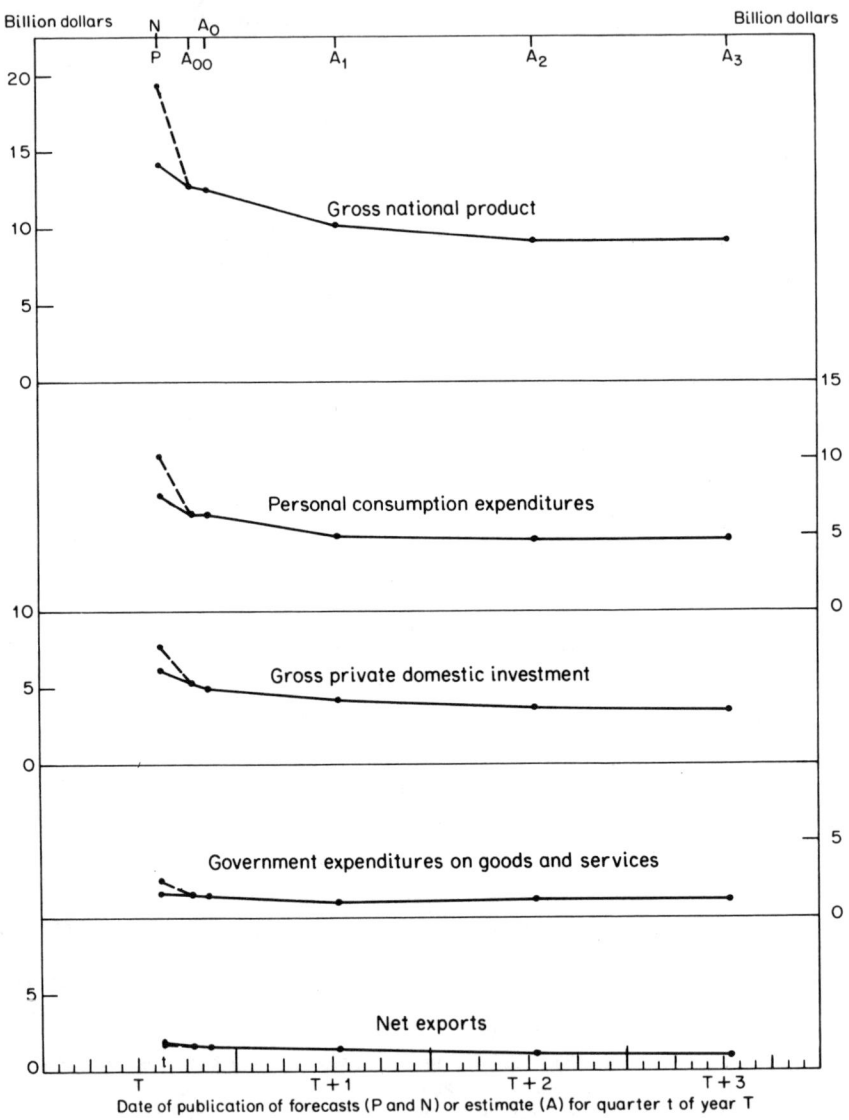

[a] See Table 6 and text for description of naive projections, forecasts, and estimates.

error statistics presented in Chart 2 and Table 6 suggest that a typical forecaster's estimates of current quarterly levels are considerably less accurate than the first official estimates of GNP, personal consumption expenditures, and gross private domestic investment. There is practically no difference, however, in the accuracy of the three estimates of government expenditures on goods and services and net exports.[26]

The root mean square error of a typical forecaster's estimates of current quarterly levels (P) and of the official estimates (A_j) of GNP and its major components for the period 1957 IV–1962 IV are plotted in Chart 2. Errors that would be made by naive model projections are also shown. The naive model (N) projects the last known quarterly value; namely, the value for the preceding quarter as published two months following the end of that quarter.

These simple projections of no change would err by the amount of the change which in fact takes place from period $t-1$ to $t+1$. To be of any value, a forecasting model should be able to predict the essential features of this change and the resulting new level of the series in period t. Consequently, predictions as well as the model generating them, could be considered worthless if their errors exceed those of the naive model N.

The statistics in Chart 2 and Table 6 show that the forecasters' estimates (P) are more accurate than the naive projections (N) and that the official estimates (A_{00} and A_0) are in turn more accurate than P for GNP and all components save one. For this component, net exports, there is almost no difference between the accuracy of N and the three sets of estimates: P, A_{00}, and A_0. In other words, neither the forecasts nor the official estimates give us very reliable current information on net exports.[27]

Provisional Estimates Compared with Extrapolations

The preceding tables and charts cover only part of the period for which estimates of gross national product and its components have been pub-

---

[26] The errors shown for the forecasts as well as the official estimates of these components reflect definitional changes in addition to statistical error (see footnote 23). This does not, however, affect comparisons between forecast and data errors. Differences in the errors arise only from differences in statistical error; the element of error due to definitional changes is the same in each set of predictions.

[27] Zellner, *A Note on Provisional Estimates,* in his study covering the 1947 II–1955 IV period, found net exports, a component estimated as a residual, to be one of the least accurate.

TABLE 6. Errors in Forecasts, Naive Model Projections, and Successive Estimates of Quarterly Levels of Gross National Product and Its Major Components, 1957 IV–1962 IV[a]

Line	Code of Forecasts and Estimates[b]	Mean Error (1)	Standard Deviation of Error (2)	Mean Absolute Error (3)	Root Mean Square Error (4)
		(billion dollars)			
	GROSS NATIONAL PRODUCT				
1	N: Naive projection of last known level	−17.5	8.3	17.5	19.3
2	P: Typical business forecast	−12.8	6.4	12.8	14.2
3	A_{00}: Advance estimates	−11.9	4.7	11.9	12.7
4	A_0: Provisional estimates	−11.6	4.7	11.6	12.5
5	A_1: First July revised estimates	−9.7	3.1	9.7	10.1
6	A_2: Second July revised estimates	−8.9	2.4	8.9	9.2
7	A_3: Third July revised estimates	−9.0	2.2	9.0	9.2
	PERSONAL CONSUMPTION EXPENDITURES				
8	N	−9.8	2.9	9.8	10.2
9	P	−6.6	3.8	6.6	7.6
10	A_{00}	−5.8	2.3	5.8	6.3
11	A_0	−6.0	2.1	6.0	6.3
12	A_1	−4.5	1.9	4.5	4.9
13	A_2	−4.4	1.6	4.4	4.7
14	A_3	−4.5	1.4	4.5	4.7
	GROSS PRIVATE DOMESTIC INVESTMENT				
15	N	−4.7	6.3	6.7	7.7
16	P	−4.5	4.2	4.8	6.1
17	A_{00}	−4.6	2.7	4.6	5.3
18	A_0	−4.2	2.6	4.2	4.9
19	A_1	−3.7	2.0	3.7	4.2
20	A_2	−3.3	1.6	3.3	3.7
21	A_3	−3.3	1.1	3.3	3.5
	GOV'T. EXPENDITURES ON GOODS AND SERVICES				
22	N	−1.6	1.8	2.0	2.4
23	P	−0.1	1.6	1.3	1.6
24	A_{00}	0.1	1.5	1.2	1.5
25	A_0	0.0	1.5	1.2	1.4
26	A_1	−0.1	1.0	0.9	1.0
27	A_2	−0.3	1.1	0.7	1.1
28	A_3	−0.3	1.0	0.7	1.1

TABLE 6. (concluded)

Line	Code of Forecasts and Estimates[b]	Mean Error (1)	Standard Deviation of Error (billion dollars) (2)	Mean Absolute Error (3)	Root Mean Square Error (4)
			NET EXPORTS		
29	N	−1.5	1.0	1.5	1.8
30	P	−1.6	1.1	1.7	1.9
31	A_{00}	−1.5	0.8	1.5	1.7
32	A_0	−1.5	0.6	1.5	1.6
33	A_1	−1.3	0.5	1.3	1.4
34	A_2	−1.1	0.2	1.1	1.1
35	A_3	−1.0	0.2	1.0	1.0

NOTE: Forecast and estimates refer to quarter t of year T.

Forecast of Estimate	Date of Publication
N	Second month of t
P	First to third month of t
A_{00}	First month of $t + 1$
A_0	Second month of $t + 1$
A_1	July, $T + 1$
A_2	July, $T + 2$
A_3	July, $T + 3$

[a]Variables are in current dollars, seasonally adjusted, at annual rates. Errors are computed as $E = P - A_n$ for forecasts and $\epsilon_j = A_j - A_n$ for the official estimates.

[b]The forecasts are from Zarnowitz' sample, set C. The advance estimates (A_{00}) are from *Economic Indicators* one month following the close of the quarter covered. Provisional estimates (A_0) are from the *Survey of Current Business* two months following the close of each quarter and the first July revised estimates (A_1) are from the following July issue of *SCB*. The second July revised estimates (A_2) are published one year later and the third July revised estimates (A_3) are published the year thereafter (see Table 1, note b).

lished on a current basis. Errors in successive estimates over the longer period 1947 II–1961 IV are summarized in Chart 3. The errors refer to estimates of both quarterly levels and of quarterly changes. The record of none of the forecasts in Zarnowitz' sample matches this period; therefore, errors in the official estimates are compared with those in naive projections of the last known quarter, or projections of "no change" (N).

Though they are widely used, the naive projections (N) provide only a minimum benchmark or standard of accuracy. The provisional data,

CHART 3. Root Mean Square Errors of Naive Projections (N) and Successive Estimates (A_j) of Quarterly Levels and Changes in Gross National Product and Its Components, 1947 II–1961 IV [a]

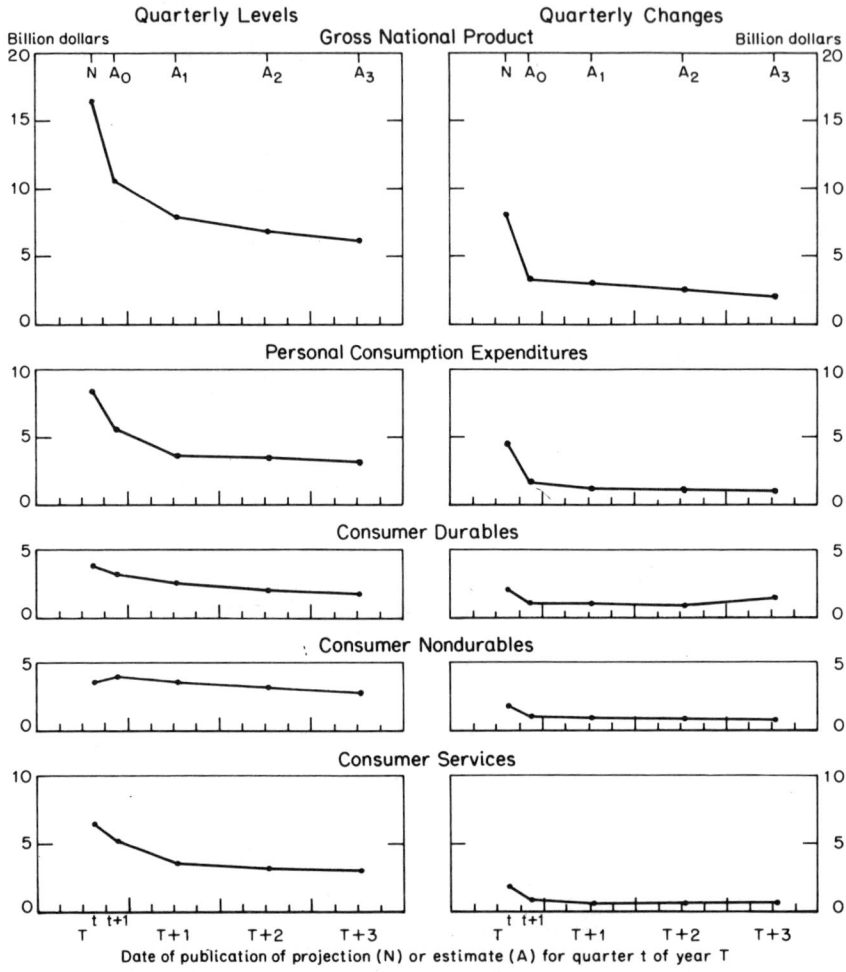

[a] See Table 7 and text for description of projections and estimates.

Relative Accuracy

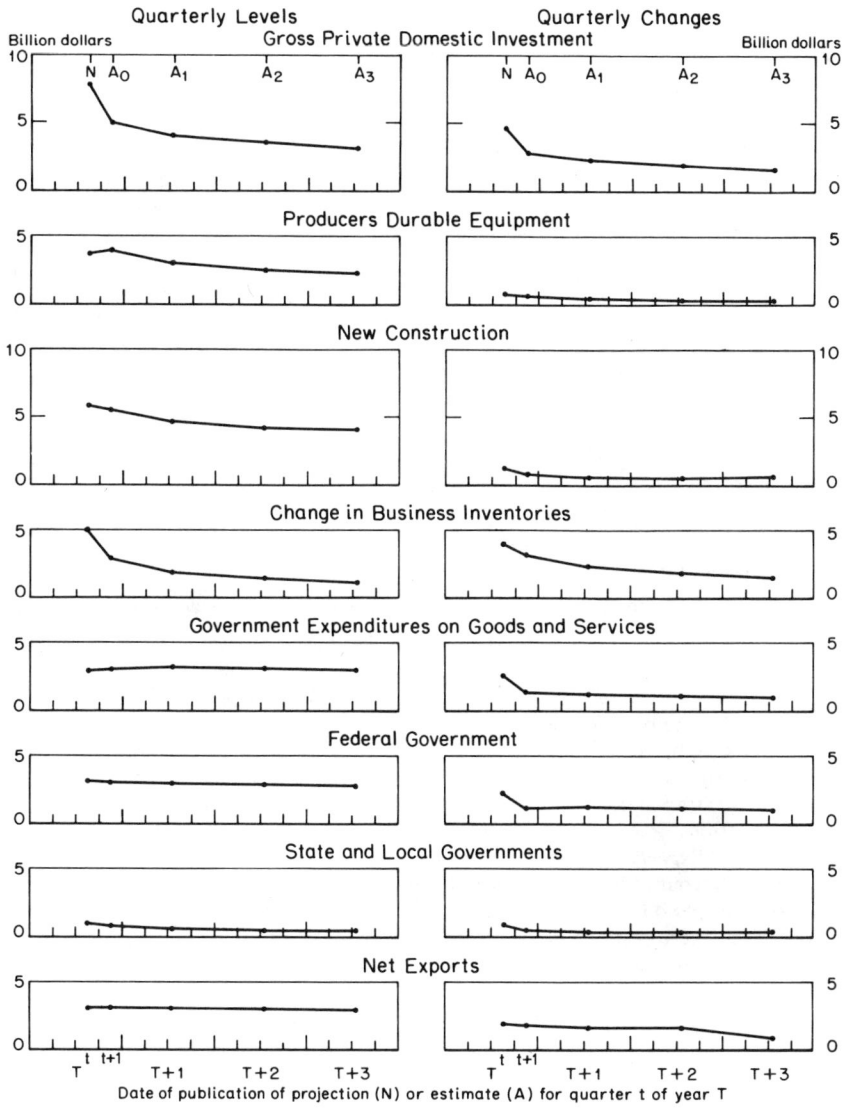

to be useful in analyzing current business conditions, should not only be more accurate than simple projections of no change; they should also accurately reflect the systematic changes in the series.[28] Errors in each of the sequence of estimates of GNP and its components are therefore compared both with the errors of N and with the errors of unbiased and efficient extrapolations, X, in Table 7 (columns 4–5 and 9–10).[29]

---

[28] A similar requirement for the accuracy of preliminary statistics is suggested by Geoffrey Moore and Julius Shiskin in *Indications of Business Expansions and Contractions,* NBER Occasional Paper 103, New York, 1967, Chapter 2, p. 17, footnote 6.

They suggest that preliminary statistics could be considered acceptable if the underlying trend of the series (the trend-cycle component) would not be altered by subsequent revisions (i.e., if the errors are merely random.)

[29] The root mean square errors of unbiased and efficient extrapolations, X, are computed for Table 7 as

$$\sqrt{M_X} = \sqrt{(1 - r^2_{A_{n_t} A_{0_{t-1}}}) S^2_{A_{n_t}}}$$

rather than

$$\sqrt{M_X} = \sqrt{(1 - r^2_{A_{n_t} A_{n_{t-1}}}) S^2_{A_{n_t}}}$$

as they were in Table 1.

The use of $A_{0_{t-1}}$ rather than $A_{n_{t-1}}$, however, takes only partial account of the fact that final data would not be available to use in projections of the value of A in period t. As a consequence, the error statistic $\sqrt{M_X}$ that is used in Table 7 would be too small and would provide too severe a standard of accuracy. If, however, the true autoregressive structure were of an order higher than the first, $\sqrt{M_X}$ would be too high.

It is unlikely, however, that the magnitude of the upward bias is sufficient to offset the downward bias. (Mincer and Zarnowitz find relatively small differences in the accuracy of extrapolations based on first order regressions and those based on higher order regressions—see "The Evaluation of Economic Forecasts," in Mincer, *Economic Forecasts and Expectations,* pp. 3–46.)

It would, of course, have been preferable to generate a series of extrapolations of the value of A in period t, each based on the history of A as it is known in period $t-1$. That is, each extrapolation (X_t) would be computed as

$$X_t = a_0 + a_1 A_{0_{t-1}},$$

where a_0 and a_1 are coefficients estimated from the regression,

$$A_{0_{t-1}} = a_0 + a_1 A_{0_{t-2}} + u_{t-1},$$

for the period 1947 I to the current quarter $t-1$.

A series of such extrapolations would require a succession of estimation, projection, and re-estimation for each quarter of the 1947–61 period and for each of the variables reviewed. While there is no denying that such a procedure would have yielded more appropriate standards of accuracy for the provisional estimates, the costs of obtaining them, in terms of the enormous amount of computations involved, were deemed too great for the purposes of this study.

TABLE 7. Errors in Naive Model Projections and Successive Estimates of Quarterly Levels and Changes in Gross National Product and Its Components, 1947 II–1961 IV
(billion dollars)

		QUARTERLY LEVELS					QUARTERLY CHANGES[b]				
					Relative Root Mean Square Error[c]					Relative Root Mean Square Error[c]	
Line	Code of Estimate[a]	Mean Error (1)	Standard Deviation of Error (2)	Root Mean Square Error (3)	RM_N (4)	RM_X (5)	Mean Error (6)	Standard Deviation of Error (7)	Root Mean Square Error (8)	RM_N (9)	RM_X (10)
					GROSS NATIONAL PRODUCT						
1	N	−13.6	9.0	16.4			−5.5	6.1	8.1		
2	A_0	−8.9	5.6	10.5	.640	1.221	−0.6	3.2	3.2	.395	.571
3	A_1	−6.1	4.8	7.7	.470	.895	−0.4	2.9	2.9	.358	.518
4	A_2	−5.3	4.2	6.7	.408	.779	−0.1	2.4	2.4	.296	.428
5	A_3	−5.0	3.6	6.1	.372	.709	−0.0	2.0	2.0	.247	.357
					PERSONAL CONSUMPTION EXPENDITURES						
6	N	−7.0	4.8	8.4			−3.3	3.0	4.5		
7	A_0	−4.4	3.3	5.5	.655	1.341	−0.7	1.4	1.6	.356	.533
8	A_1	−2.1	2.8	3.5	.417	.854	−0.3	1.2	1.2	.267	.400
9	A_2	−1.7	3.0	3.4	.405	.829	−0.2	1.1	1.1	.244	.367
10	A_3	−1.5	2.7	3.1	.369	.756	−0.2	1.0	1.0	.222	.333
					CONSUMER DURABLES						
11	N	−2.9	2.4	3.8			−0.5	1.9	2.0		
12	A_0	−2.6	1.8	3.2	.842	1.333	−0.2	1.0	1.0	.500	.526
13	A_1	−1.7	1.8	2.5	.658	1.042	−0.1	1.0	1.0	.500	.526
14	A_2	−1.3	1.5	2.0	.625	.833	−0.0	0.9	0.9	.450	.474
15	A_3	−1.1	1.4	1.7	.531	.708	0.0	1.1	1.1	.550	.579

TABLE 7. (continued)

Line	Code of Estimate[a]	QUARTERLY LEVELS					QUARTERLY CHANGES[b]			
		Mean Error (1)	Standard Deviation of Error (2)	Root Mean Square Error (3)	Relative Root Mean Square Error[c]		Mean Error (6)	Standard Deviation of Error (7)	Root Mean Square Error (8)	Relative Root Mean Square Error[c]
					RM_N (4)	RM_X (5)				RM_N (9)	RM_X (10)

CONSUMER NONDURABLES

16	N	2.3	2.8	3.6							
17	A_0	3.3	2.3	4.0	1.111	1.739	−1.2	1.4	1.8	.556	.714
18	A_1	3.1	2.0	3.6	1.000	1.565	−0.2	1.0	1.0	.500	.643
19	A_2	2.6	1.8	3.2	.889	1.391	0.0	0.9	0.9	.444	.571
20	A_3	2.3	1.7	2.8	.778	1.217	−0.0	0.8	0.8	.389	.500
							−0.1	0.7	0.7		

CONSUMER SERVICES

21	N	−6.4	1.4	6.5			−1.6	0.7	1.8		
22	A_0	−5.1	1.4	5.3	.815	2.650	−0.3	0.7	0.8	.444	1.143
23	A_1	−3.5	0.8	3.6	.554	1.800	−0.2	0.6	0.6	.333	.857
24	A_2	−3.0	1.2	3.2	.492	1.600	−0.1	0.6	0.6	.333	.857
25	A_3	−2.7	1.4	3.0	.462	1.500	−0.0	0.6	0.6	.333	.857

GROSS PRIVATE DOMESTIC INVESTMENT

26	N	−4.3	6.5	7.8			−0.8	4.7	4.7		
27	A_0	−3.4	3.5	4.9	.628	.778	0.0	2.7	2.7	.574	.574
28	A_1	−3.1	2.5	4.0	.513	.635	−0.1	2.3	2.3	.489	.489
29	A_2	−2.8	2.0	3.5	.449	.556	0.1	1.9	1.9	.404	.404
30	A_3	−2.8	1.3	3.1	.397	.492	0.0	1.6	1.6	.340	.340

TABLE 7. (continued)

Line	Code of Estimate[a]	QUARTERLY LEVELS					QUARTERLY CHANGES[b]				
		Mean Error (1)	Standard Deviation of Error (2)	Root Mean Square Error (3)	Relative Root Mean Square Error[c]		Mean Error (6)	Standard Deviation of Error (7)	Root Mean Square Error (8)	Relative Root Mean Square Error[c]	
					RM_N (4)	RM_X (5)				RM_N (9)	RM_X (10)
				PRODUCERS' DURABLE EQUIPMENT							
31	N	1.6	3.4	3.7			−0.2	1.1	1.1		
32	A_0	2.2	3.2	3.9	1.054	1.147	0.3	0.9	0.9	.818	.818
33	A_1	1.0	2.8	2.9	.784	.853	0.0	0.7	0.7	.636	.636
34	A_2	0.7	2.4	2.5	.676	.735	−0.0	0.6	0.6	.545	.545
35	A_3	0.6	2.2	2.3	.622	.676	−0.0	0.6	0.6	.545	.545
				NEW CONSTRUCTION							
36	N	−5.1	2.9	5.8			−0.4	1.1	1.2		
37	A_0	−4.8	2.8	5.5	.948	2.115	−0.1	0.7	0.7	.583	.700
38	A_1	−3.9	2.3	4.6	.793	1.769	0.0	0.6	0.6	.500	.600
39	A_2	−3.6	2.0	4.2	.724	1.615	0.1	0.5	0.5	.417	.500
40	A_3	−3.5	1.9	4.0	.690	1.538	0.1	0.6	0.6	.500	.600
				CHANGE IN BUSINESS INVENTORIES							
41	N	−0.7	5.0	5.0			−0.1	3.9	3.9		
42	A_0	−0.8	2.7	2.8	.560	.667	−0.2	3.1	3.1	.795	.795
43	A_1	−0.3	1.8	1.8	.360	.428	−0.1	2.3	2.3	.590	.590
44	A_2	0.0	1.4	1.4	.280	.333	0.0	1.9	1.8	.462	.462
45	A_3	0.1	1.1	1.1	.220	.262	0.0	1.5	1.5	.385	.385

TABLE 7. (continued)

Line	Code of Estimate[a]	QUARTERLY LEVELS					QUARTERLY CHANGES[b]				
		Mean Error (1)	Standard Deviation of Error (2)	Root Mean Square Error (3)	Relative Root Mean Square Error[c]		Mean Error (6)	Standard Deviation of Error (7)	Root Mean Square Error (8)	Relative Root Mean Square Error[c]	
					RM_N (4)	RM_X (5)				RM_N (9)	RM_X (10)
		GOVERNMENT EXPENDITURES ON GOODS AND SERVICES									
46	N	0.7	2.2	2.9			−1.5	2.2	2.6		
47	A_0	2.1	2.2	3.0	1.034	1.154	−0.1	1.3	1.3	.500	.867
48	A_1	2.3	2.2	3.2	1.103	1.231	−0.0	1.2	1.2	.462	.800
49	A_2	2.3	2.1	3.1	1.069	1.192	−0.0	1.1	1.1	.423	.733
50	A_3	2.2	2.1	3.0	1.034	1.154	−0.0	1.0	1.0	.385	.667
		FEDERAL GOVERNMENT									
51	N	1.3	2.8	3.1			−0.8	2.2	2.3		
52	A_0	2.0	2.2	3.0	.968	1.154	−0.1	1.1	1.1	.478	.786
53	A_1	2.0	2.1	2.9	.935	1.115	−0.0	1.2	1.2	.522	.857
54	A_2	1.9	2.0	2.8	.903	1.077	−0.0	1.1	1.1	.478	.786
55	A_3	1.8	2.0	2.7	.871	1.038	−0.0	1.0	1.0	.437	.714
		STATE AND LOCAL GOVERNMENTS									
56	N	−0.5	0.7	0.9			−0.7	0.4	0.8		
57	A_0	0.1	0.7	0.7	.778	1.000	−0.0	0.4	0.4	.500	1.000
58	A_1	0.3	0.4	0.5	.556	.714	−0.0	0.3	0.3	.375	.750
59	A_2	0.4	0.2	0.4	.444	.571	0.0	0.3	0.3	.375	.750
60	A_3	0.3	0.2	0.4	.444	.571	0.0	0.3	0.3	.375	.750

TABLE 7. (concluded)

Line	Code of Estimate[a]	QUARTERLY LEVELS					QUARTERLY CHANGES[b]			
		Mean Error (1)	Standard Deviation of Error (2)	Root Mean Square Error (3)	Relative Root Mean Square Error[c]		Mean Error (6)	Standard Deviation of Error (7)	Root Mean Square Error (8)	Relative Root Mean Square Error[c]	
					RM_N (4)	RM_X (5)				RM_N (9)	RM_X (10)

NET EXPORTS

61	N	−2.7	1.6	3.1	1.000	2.067	−0.1	1.9	1.8	.944	1.700
62	A_0	−2.6	1.6	3.1	.968	2.000	−0.1	1.7	1.7	.889	1.600
63	A_1	−2.6	1.4	3.0	.935	1.933	−0.2	1.6	1.6	.889	1.600
64	A_2	−2.5	1.5	2.9	.903	1.867	−0.2	1.6	1.6	.444	.800
65	A_3	−2.4	1.5	2.8			−0.0	0.8	0.8		

[a]Estimates refer to quarter t of year T. The date of publication and notation is:

Date Published

Second month of t N: Naive projection of last known quarterly level ($A_{0_{t-1}}$)
    A_0: Provisional estimates
Second month of t + 1 A_1: First July revised estimates
July, $T + 1$ A_2: Second July revised estimates
July, $T + 2$ A_3: Third July revised estimates
July, $T + 3$

[b]The first estimates of quarter-to-quarter change are not simply the change in the provisional estimates of levels, $A_{0_t} - A_{0_{t-1}}$. In some cases $A_{0_{t-1}}$ has been revised by the time the estimate of A_{0_t} is made. For example, the first estimates of change from the first to second quarter of a year would be $A_{0_t} - A_{1_{t-1}}$. These current basis revisions were discontinued in 1954 because they were so often offset by the first July revisions. The changes used here are the estimates of change and not the change in a given set of level estimates ($A_{j_t} - A_{j_{t-1}}$).

[c]Relative root mean square roots RM_N and RM_X are $RM_N = \sqrt{M_j}/\sqrt{M_N}$ and $RM_X = \sqrt{M_j}/\sqrt{M_X}$; where $\sqrt{M_j}$ is the root mean square error of each set of official estimates ($j = 0, \ldots, 3$), $\sqrt{M_N}$ is the root mean square of naive projections, and $\sqrt{M_X}$ is the root mean square error of unbiased and efficient extrapolations. $\sqrt{M_X}$ is computed

$$\sqrt{M_X} = \sqrt{(1 - r^2_{A_{n_t}, A_{0_{t-1}}})S^2_{A_{n_t}}}.$$

The provisional estimates of quarterly levels are on the whole superior to N, but their errors exceed those of X (compare the initial entries in columns 4 and 5 in Table 7). The early data on quarterly changes, however, are substantially more accurate. The errors in levels exceed those in changes in all four major sectors, as well as in all but one of the detailed components. This is true both in terms of the absolute errors (compare the statistics in columns 1–3 with those in columns 6–8, respectively) and in terms of the relative errors (columns 4–5 compared with columns 9–10, respectively). The only exception is in estimates of the change in business inventories.

Although there is considerable bias in the initial estimates of quarterly levels, it appears to be very small in the change estimates.[30] Even so, the bias in the provisional estimates of quarterly changes in expenditures on producers' durable equipment, the change in business inventories, and net exports is greater than that in naive projections of "no change" (column 6).

The early figures are more efficient than naive projections for GNP and most of the components, but there are some exceptions. For example, the first estimates of consumer services (quarterly levels and changes), new construction (levels), and net exports (levels), as well as state and local government expenditures on goods and services (levels and changes) are only about as efficient as N.

To sum up, errors in the provisional estimates of quarterly changes in GNP and its components are on the average about 60 per cent as large as the errors in naive projections of no change (N) and about 90 per cent as large as the errors in unbiased and efficient extrapolations (X). Thus, one would have been about 10 per cent more accurate using the early quarterly change data than in relying on very accurate extrapolations (X).

The early data for levels are less accurate. We have seen that the provisional estimates were not much more accurate than an average of forecasters' estimates of current annual levels during the 1953–62 period,

---

[30] The fact that the revisions affect levels considerably more than changes is the reason why errors in absolute rather than in percentage changes are used in Table 7. If, for example, the initial estimate of change were from 100 in quarter $t-1$ to 105 in quarter t and the revised estimate, from 105 in quarter $t-1$ to 110 in quarter t, the change in both sets of estimates, in absolute terms, is 5. In percentage terms, however, the initial estimate of a 5 per cent change would appear to overestimate the revised change of 4.8 per cent.

even though the forecasts are published three to four months earlier than the official figures. Comparisons with typical forecasts of quarterly data are more favorable. The provisional estimates were roughly 15 per cent more accurate than a typical forecaster's estimates of current quarterly levels for 1957 IV–1962 IV. Over the longer period 1947 II–1961 IV, however, errors in the early level data were on the whole larger than the errors in unbiased and efficient extrapolations.

IV

Gains in Accuracy from Additional Information

Gains Through Successive Revisions

Each successive forecast and estimate contains more information relevant to the period covered than the preceding one. Does the additional information lead to a steady reduction in error? More specifically, is A_j a more accurate prediction of A_n than is A_{j-1}? The error statistics shown thus far indicate that on the whole the answer is yes. Revised forecasts and estimates show a reduction in over-all error achieved by both a reduction in bias and an increase in efficiency.

In the sequence of forecasts and estimates of annual levels of GNP and its major components, the greatest gains in accuracy occur in the forecasts (see Chart 1). Theil finds a similar result for the Dutch data. The official Dutch forecasts show a much larger reduction in error than do the official estimates.[31] One would expect this to be the case. New information about the early part of year T, which would induce a revision in a forecast, prepared in year $T - 1$, of the value of the variable in year T, amounts to considerably more than the increments of information that become available after year T has passed and which would cause revisions in the official estimates.

In the case of quarterly data, Table 7 shows that there is a fairly steady reduction in error both in the estimates of levels and of changes. Moreover, except for estimates of the levels of government expenditures on goods and services, the revised estimates are more accurate than N for those components whose provisional estimates were less accurate.

[31] Theil, *Applied Economic Forecasting*, Chapter 5.

Gains in Accuracy 49

Table 8 shows how rapidly errors in the provisional estimates of quarterly levels and changes are reduced through successive revision. For this purpose, the total error eliminated is measured by the root mean square error of the provisional estimates ($\sqrt{M_0}$). $\sqrt{M_0}$ is reduced by the three annual July revisions to $\sqrt{M_1}$, $\sqrt{M_2}$, and $\sqrt{M_3}$ and then eliminated by the 1965 major benchmark revision. The percentage reduction in $\sqrt{M_0}$ resulting from each of these revisions is given in the table.

It is clear that major benchmark revisions are the most important. As a rough average, nearly 60 per cent of the error in the initial estimates remains until these revisions occur.[32] The first July revision tends to be the most important of the three annual revisions, eliminating as much as one-quarter to one-third of the error in levels. It has somewhat less effect on the errors in changes.

The revisions do not reduce errors in every case. For example, no reduction is shown in the errors in estimates of levels in government expenditures on goods and services, nor is there any decrease after the second annual July revision in the errors in estimating quarterly changes in expenditures on consumer durables and new construction.

It might seem from Table 8 that it takes a rather long time to achieve substantial reductions in the errors. Table 9 explores the possibility that the errors could have been reduced more rapidly. Each successive revision is correlated with the errors eliminated in subsequent revisions. Correlations significantly different from zero would suggest that subsequent revisions could be predicted from earlier revisions. If this were the case, linear adjustments of the revisions could result in a more rapid reduction of error. The evidence in Table 9, however, indicates no strong potential for such corrections. Most of the correlations are not statistically different from zero and, but for a few exceptions, those that are significant are fairly weak. Nevertheless, the preponderance of negative signs is striking and suggests that small (large) early revisions are likely to be followed by larger (smaller) revisions.

[32] The reduction in error attributed in Table 8 to benchmark revisions was achieved through two major revisions. Errors in the data for the 1947 II–1954 IV period were primarily eliminated by the major revision of 1958 and errors in the later data, 1955 I–1961 IV, were eliminated by the 1965 revision. Although the figures for the earlier period were also revised in 1965, the statistical revisions of these data were fairly small (for GNP, they average $2.5 billion, without regard to sign).

TABLE 8. Per Cent of Error in Provisional Estimates of Quarterly Levels and Changes in Gross National Product and Its Components Eliminated in Each Successive Revision, 1947 II–1961 IV[a]

Line	Variable	QUARTERLY LEVELS				QUARTERLY CHANGES			
		Annual July Revisions			Major Benchmark Revisions[b]	Annual July Revisions			Major Benchmark Revisions[b]
		First (1)	Second (2)	Third (3)	(4)	First (5)	Second (6)	Third (7)	(8)
1	Gross National Product	26.7%	9.5%	5.7%	58.1%	9.4%	15.6%	12.5%	62.5%
2	Personal Consumption Expenditures	36.4	1.8	5.4	56.4	25.0	6.2	6.2	62.5
3	Durables	21.9	15.6	9.4	53.1	0.0	10.0	c	c
4	Nondurables	10.0	10.0	10.0	70.0	10.0	10.0	10.0	70.0
5	Services	32.1	7.5	3.8	56.6	25.0	10.0	0.0	75.0
6	Gross Private Domestic Investment	18.4	10.2	8.2	63.3	14.8	14.8	11.1	59.2
7	Producers' durable equipment	25.6	10.2	5.1	59.0	22.2	11.1	0.0	66.7
8	New construction	16.4	7.3	3.6	72.7	14.3	14.3	c	c
9	Change in business inventories	35.7	14.3	10.7	39.3	25.8	16.1	9.7	48.4
10	Gov't. Expenditures on Goods and Services	c	c	c	c	c	7.7	7.7	76.9
11	Federal	3.3	3.3	3.3	90.0	7.7	0.0	9.1	90.9
12	State and local	28.6	14.3	0.0	57.1	25.0	0.0	0.0	75.0
13	Net Exports	3.2	3.2	3.2	90.3	5.9	0.0	47.0	47.0

[a] Percentage of error eliminated in the first July revision is computed as $100 \times \left(\frac{\sqrt{M_0} - \sqrt{M_1}}{\sqrt{M_0}}\right)$; in the second July revision, $100 \times \left(\frac{\sqrt{M_1} - \sqrt{M_2}}{\sqrt{M_0}}\right)$; in the third July revision, $100 \times \left(\frac{\sqrt{M_2} - \sqrt{M_3}}{\sqrt{M_0}}\right)$; and in the 1965 major benchmark revision, $100 \times \left(\frac{\sqrt{M_3}}{\sqrt{M_0}}\right)$, where $\sqrt{M_0}$ is the root mean square error of A_0, $\sqrt{M_1}$ is the root mean square error of A_1, etc. The root mean square errors are from Table 7.

[b] Statistical revisions only. Errors eliminated by the 1958 major benchmark revision as well as the 1965 revision are included in these figures.

[c] The root mean square error was not reduced by these revisions (see Table 7).

There are some difficulties, however, in looking only at the reductions in the root mean square error statistics as shown in Table 8 to determine whether or not the revisions have reduced error. For example, reduction in an unusually large error may more than offset small increases in several errors. Moreover, cases in which a revision does not occur are included and would appear as no reduction of error in the summary statistics.

Each revision in the estimates of quarterly changes is classified in Table 10 according to whether it reduces or increases the previous error. That is, the error is considered reduced if the jth revision makes $\triangle A_j$ a more accurate estimate of $\triangle A_n$ (the quarterly change as indicated by the 1965 statistically revised estimates) than was $\triangle A_{j-1}$. There are five possible outcomes of such comparisons: the revision may (1) make $\triangle A_j$ exactly equal to $\triangle A_n$; (2) be in the correct direction but not large enough so $\triangle A_j$ is between $\triangle A_{j-1}$ and $\triangle A_n$; (3) overshoot but nonetheless bring $\triangle A_j$ closer to $\triangle A_n$ than was $\triangle A_{j-1}$; (4) overshoot with the result that $\triangle A_j$ is the same or further from $\triangle A_n$ than was $\triangle A_{j-1}$; and (5) be in the wrong direction and make $\triangle A_j$ even further from $\triangle A_n$ than was $\triangle A_{j-1}$. The first three outcomes are successes inasmuch as they result in reductions of errors; the last two are considered failures. Cases in which a revision does not occur (i.e., $\triangle A_j = \triangle A_{j-1}$) are excluded from the counts.

The gains in accuracy suggested by Table 7 appear more modest in Table 10. As we could expect from the fact that the summary statistics of error are reduced, revisions decrease error more than 50 per cent of the time (Table 10, column 2). But not much more. An average over all of the detailed components and all of the revisions is that 60 per cent of the revisions decreased error, but 40 per cent of them increased it.[33]

Revisions of the advance estimates (R_0) are included in Table 10. These revisions, published only one month after the advance figures appear, are least successful of all. Only about one-half of them reduce error. In other words, only one-half of the advance estimates were closer to the final (1965) figures than the provisional estimates were.[34]

---

[33] Theil (*Applied Economic Forecasting*, p. 146) presents similar results for the Dutch data. About 64 per cent of the revisions in estimates of annual change reduce error. He finds revisions of forecasts show about the same success; on the average, 66 per cent reduce error.

[34] Stekler, *Data Revisions and Economic Forecasting*, Table 5, shows similar results for comparisons of the advance and provisional estimates with earlier data—that available in July 1964. His comparisons cover the 1956–64 period.

TABLE 9. Coefficients of Correlation Between Successive Revisions and Errors Eliminated in Subsequent Revisions of Estimates of Quarterly Levels and Changes in Gross National Product and Its Components[a], 1947 II–1961 IV

		ANNUAL JULY REVISIONS					
		Quarterly Levels			Quarterly Changes		
Line	Variable	$r_{R_1\epsilon_1}$ (1)	$r_{R_2\epsilon_2}$ (2)	$r_{R_3\epsilon_3}$ (3)	$r_{R_1\epsilon_1}$ (4)	$r_{R_2\epsilon_2}$ (5)	$r_{R_3\epsilon_3}$ (6)
1	Gross National Product	−.0823	.0532	.0512	.0425	−.1432	−.2176
2	Personal Consumption Expenditures	.0641	−.2925*	.1505	.2797*	−.1585	.1837
3	Durables	−.3594	−.1587	−.2082	−.3139*	.1645	−.5605**
4	Nondurables	−.0984	−.1005	−.0099	−.1892	−.1032	−.2646*
5	Services	−.2003	−.7401**	−.4950**	−.0135	−.1821	−.4125**
6	Gross Private Domestic Investment	−.0429	.0320	.0701	−.1809	−.0540	−.0618
7	Producers' durables	.1303	.1451	−.0442	−.0151	−.2040	−.4607**
8	New construction	.1332	.4108**	.1894	−.1914	−.0241	−.3117*
9	Change in business inventories	−.0453	.0740	−.1357	−.0651	−.0229	−.0686
10	Gov't. Expend. on Goods and Services	−.2464	−.0566	−.1565	−.4184**	.0345	−.2248
11	Federal government	−.1482	.0118	−.1188	−.4713**	−.0266	−.2153
12	State and local governments	−.0874	−.0689	−.3590**	−.3539**	−.0770	−.3407**
13	Net Exports of Goods and Services	.0267	−.3122*	−.2149	−.0833	−.1315	.0842

NOTE: * denotes statistically different from zero at the 5 per cent level; ** denotes statistically different from zero at the 1 per cent level.

Date Published	
July, $T+1$	First July revisions:
July, $T+2$	Second July revisions:
July, $T+3$	Third July revisions:

The remaining error is defined $\epsilon_1 = A_1 - A_n$, $\epsilon_2 = A_2 - A_n$, and $\epsilon_3 = A_3 - A_n$.

$R_1 = A_0 - A_1$
$R_2 = A_1 - A_2$
$R_3 = A_2 - A_3$

[a] The provisional estimates (A_0) refer to quarter t of year T. The date and notation of the revisions and errors are:

TABLE 10. Successive Revisions in Estimates of Quarterly Change in Gross National Product and Its Components Classified According to Success or Failure of Revisions[a]

Line	Description of Revisions	Interval Between ΔA_j and ΔA_{j+1}	Period Covered	Number of Revisions[b] (1)	Percentage Distribution of Revisions According to Effect on Previous Error		Probability of At Least As Many Error Reductions[e] (4)
					Error Reduced (2)	Error Increased (3) (per cent)	
			GROSS NATIONAL PRODUCT				
1	R_0: ΔA_{00} to ΔA_0	1 mo.	1950–61	42	52.4	47.6	.383
2	R_1: ΔA_0 to ΔA_1	8–17 mos.	1947–61	59	55.9	44.1	.184
3	R_2: ΔA_1 to ΔA_2	12 mos.	1947–61	56	75.0	25.0	.001
4	R_3: ΔA_2 to ΔA_3	12 mos.	1947–61	57	68.4	31.6	.003
			PERSONAL CONSUMPTION EXPENDITURES				
5	R_0	1 mo.	1950–61	44	59.1	40.9	.127
6	R_1	8–17 mos.	1947–61	59	59.3	40.7	.078
7	R_2	12 mos.	1947–61	57	52.6	47.4	.349
8	R_3	12 mos.	1947–61	53	56.6	43.4	.171
			CONSUMER DURABLES				
9	R_0	1 mo.	1950–61	39	53.8	46.2	.320
10	R_1	8–17 mos.	1947–61	53	45.2	54.8	.756
11	R_2	12 mos.	1947–61	50	56.0	44.0	.202
12	R_3	12 mos.	1947–61	39	53.9	46.1	.320
			CONSUMER NONDURABLES				
13	R_0	1 mo.	1950–61	42	45.2	54.8	.734
14	R_1	8–17 mos.	1947–61	46	56.5	43.5	.192
15	R_2	12 mos.	1947–61	51	66.7	33.3	.009
16	R_3	12 mos.	1947–61	46	45.7	54.3	.730
			CONSUMER SERVICES				
17	R_0	1 mo.	1950–61	41	70.7	29.3	.004
18	R_1	8–17 mos.	1947–61	56	69.6	30.4	.002
19	R_2	12 mos.	1947–61	48	56.2	43.8	.197
20	R_3	12 mos.	1947–61	48	58.3	41.7	.127
			GROSS PRIVATE DOMESTIC INVESTMENT				
21	R_0	1 mo.	1950–61	43	41.9	58.1	.859
22	R_1	8–17 mos.	1947–61	55	63.6	36.4	.022
23	R_2	12 mos.	1947–61	58	58.6	41.4	.096
24	R_3	12 mos.	1947–61	56	60.7	39.3	.056
			PRODUCERS' DURABLE EQUIPMENT				
25	R_0	1 mo.	1952–61	22	54.5	45.5	.343
26	R_1	8–17 mos.	1947–61	52	53.8	46.2	.293
27	R_2	12 mos.	1947–61	49	61.3	38.7	.060
28	R_3	12 mos.	1947–61	41	46.4	53.6	.683

TABLE 10. (concluded)

Line	Description of Revisions	Interval Between ΔA_j and ΔA_{j+1}	Period Covered	Number of Revisions[b] (1)	Percentage Distribution of Revisions According to Effect on Previous Error		Probability of At Least As Many Error Reductions[c] (4)
					Error Reduced (2)	Error Increased (3) (per cent)	
			NEW CONSTRUCTION				
29	R_0	1 mo.	1952–61	23	34.8	65.2	.930
30	R_1	8–17 mos.	1947–61	56	62.5	37.5	.017
31	R_2	12 mos.	1947–61	41	53.7	46.3	.324
32	R_3	12 mos.	1947–61	25	60.0	40.0	.165
			CHANGE IN BUSINESS INVENTORIES				
33	R_0	1 mo.	1952–61	35	37.1	62.9	.937
34	R_1	8–17 mos.	1947–61	54	61.1	38.9	.052
35	R_2	12 mos.	1947–61	58	62.0	38.0	.034
36	R_3	12 mos.	1947–61	57	68.4	31.6	.003
			GOV'T. EXPENDITURES ON GOODS AND SERVICES				
37	R_0	1 mo.	1950–61	45	48.9	51.1	.562
38	R_1	8–17 mos.	1947–61	57	54.4	45.6	.257
39	R_2	12 mos.	1947–61	50	60.0	40.0	.081
40	R_3	12 mos.	1947–61	44	52.3	47.7	.386
			FEDERAL GOVERNMENT				
41	R_0	1 mo.	1953–61	34	55.9	44.1	.252
42	R_1	8–17 mos.	1947–61	54	40.7	59.3	.914
43	R_2	12 mos.	1947–61	50	54.0	46.0	.290
44	R_3	12 mos.	1947–61	36	52.8	47.2	.374
			STATE AND LOCAL GOVERNMENTS				
45	R_0	1 mo.	1953–61	17	52.9	47.1	.415
46	R_1	8–17 mos.	1947–61	50	54.0	46.0	.290
47	R_2	12 mos.	1947–61	48	64.5	35.5	.022
48	R_3	12 mos.	1947–61	42	57.1	42.9	.112
			NET EXPORTS				
49	R_0	1 mo.	1950–61	36	58.3	41.7	.163
50	R_1	8–17 mos.	1947–61	56	60.6	39.4	.056
51	R_2	12 mos.	1947–61	46	56.5	43.5	.192
52	R_3	12 mos.	1947–61	36	58.3	41.7	.163

[a] See Table 7, note b for description of the changes used.
[b] Excludes cases in which no revision occurs (i.e., $\Delta A_j = \Delta A_j{-}1$).
[c] Based on the proportion of all revisions accounted for by the number resulting in error reductions. Probabilities are taken from NBER tables of Cumulative Binomial Probability Distributions.

Gains in Accuracy

The results in Table 10 (as well as in Tables 5 and 6) suggest that revisions of the advance estimates after only one month (R_0) may not be worth making. They are often reversed by the revisions made the following July (R_1). Moreover, the increases in accuracy resulting from these early revisions (R_0) are relatively small on the average and may not outweigh their costs.

Although there are a few exceptions, revisions which occur the following July (R_1) are considerably more successful. For more components, the second July revisions (R_2) are even more successful, though the third July revisions (R_3) are somewhat less so.

In most cases, however, the per cent of revisions reducing error is not strikingly over 50 per cent and it might therefore be contended that the results arise merely from chance. Suppose this contention were correct and that the revisions are random in the sense that they are as likely to increase error as to reduce it. What then would be the probabilities of observing at least as many error reductions as those found in column 2? The probabilities are given in column 4 of the table.[35] For these sample sizes (column 1), it would be necessary for the revisions to reduce error at least two-thirds of the time in order for there to be a smaller than 1 per cent probability that the results arise merely from chance. Consequently, in very few cases (6 lines out of the 52 lines of the table) would we reject, at the 1 per cent level, the hypothesis that the revisions are as likely to increase as to reduce error. The hypothesis would, however, be rejected at higher significance levels: it would be rejected at the 20 per cent level in 28 of the 52 cases; at the 33 per cent level, in 37 cases; and at the 50 per cent level, in 43 cases.

Since in general we would surely be willing to accept a greater than 1 per cent probability—indeed, up to 50 per cent—that the results arise merely from chance, we conclude that the three annual July revisions were on the whole successful, but revisions of the advance estimates after only one month were considerably less so. In terms of

---

[35] Some of the assumptions underlying the use here of the binomial distribution are not met and therefore the probabilities in Table 10 should be viewed with reservation. Most important is the assumption that the revisions are independent—both with respect to time (i.e., the jth revision of the estimate of change from period t to $t+1$, $R_{j_{t+1}}$, is unrelated to R_{j_t}, the revision of the change from period $t-1$ to t) and to each other (i.e., R_{j_t} is unrelated to R_{j+1_t}). There are a few small significant correlations between R_{j_t} and $R_{j_{t+1}}$ and between $R_{j_{t+1}}$ and R_{j+1_t}, but there is no widespread indication of strong interdependence among the revisions.

the *magnitude* of error reduced, the three annual July revisions eliminated about 40 per cent of the error in the provisional estimates that is due to incomplete primary data. The major part of this error remains until a major benchmark revision occurs.

Gains Over Time

One might expect the accuracy of the early GNP statistics to have improved over the years—partly as a return from the improvements throughout the postwar period in up-to-date reporting of economic statistics and in the mechanics of data processing and partly from the cumulated experience with past errors in the early GNP data. A major aim of Stekler's paper was to determine whether or not the accuracy of the provisional estimates has in fact improved.[36] As noted earlier, he compares the accuracy of the provisional estimates of quarterly change in GNP and its components during the 1956 I–1964 I period with that shown by Zellner for the 1947 II–1955 IV period and concludes the quality of the early figures has improved.

We have seen, however, that the errors in the early data resemble extrapolation errors. This finding raises the possibility that the apparent increase in accuracy may have come merely because many GNP series were smoother in the latter part of the postwar period and could be extrapolated more accurately. If this were the case, the apparent improvement would be unlikely to persist throughout any future periods in which the variables display greater fluctuations. Thus evidence of a genuine improvement in the early statistics would require a decline in their errors relative to extrapolation errors.

A second question arises from the fact that both Zellner's and Stekler's studies include as "final" data estimates that have not been subject to a major benchmark revision. Zellner compared the provisional estimates with data revised through July 1956 and Stekler compared them with data revised through July 1964. The final data for both studies were altered by the major benchmark revisions of 1958 and 1965. Since we have seen that the benchmark revisions are the most important of the revisions (cf. Table 8), an obvious question is whether Stekler's conclusions would hold if the initial estimates for both the early and later periods were compared with benchmark revised estimates.

[36] Stekler, *Data Revisions and Economic Forecasting*.

TABLE 11. Errors in Provisional Estimates of Quarterly Levels and Changes in Gross National Product and Its Components, 1947–54 Compared with 1955–61 [a]
(billion dollars)

			Quarterly Levels				Quarterly Changes			
Line	Variable	Period Covered	Mean Error (1)	Standard Deviation of Error (2)	Root Mean Square Error (3)	Relative Root Mean Square Error[b] (4)	Mean Error (5)	Standard Deviation of Error (6)	Root Mean Square Error (7)	Relative Root Mean Square Error[b] (8)
1	Gross National Product	1947–54	−5.0	3.9	6.3	1.125	−1.0	3.8	3.9	.848
2		1955–61	−12.8	4.6	13.6	2.386	−0.4	2.9	2.9	.483
3	Personal Consumption Expenditures	1947–54	−2.6	3.3	4.1	1.139	−0.9	1.4	1.7	.500
4		1955–61	−6.4	2.0	6.7	3.190	−0.5	1.4	1.5	.714
5	Durables	1947–54	−2.0	1.5	2.5	1.190	−0.2	0.6	0.7	.350
6		1955–61	−3.3	2.0	3.8	2.375	−0.2	1.1	1.1	.733
7	Nondurables	1947–54	4.5	2.2	5.0	2.941	−0.3	1.2	1.2	.706
8		1955–61	2.0	1.6	2.6	2.889	−0.1	0.8	.8	1.000
9	Services	1947–54	−5.0	1.1	5.1	10.200	−0.4	0.8	0.9	1.125
10		1955–61	−5.2	1.8	5.5	11.000	−0.2	0.6	0.6	1.200
11	Gross Private Domestic Investment	1947–54	−2.4	3.9	4.6	1.022	−0.1	3.1	3.0	.625
12		1955–61	−4.6	2.6	5.2	1.209	0.2	2.2	2.2	.478
13	Producers' Durables	1947–54	4.5	2.2	4.9	4.900	0.3	1.0	1.0	.909
14		1955–61	−0.3	2.1	2.1	1.909	0.3	0.7	0.8	.727
15	New Construction	1947–54	−6.5	1.6	6.7	6.091	−0.2	0.7	0.7	.700
16		1955–61	−2.9	2.7	3.9	3.900	−0.0	0.7	0.7	.875

TABLE 11. (concluded)

Line	Variable	Period Covered	Quarterly Levels				Quarterly Changes			
			Mean Error (1)	Standard Deviation of Error (2)	Root Mean Square Error (3)	Relative Root Mean Square Error[b] (4)	Mean Error (5)	Standard Deviation of Error (6)	Root Mean Square Error (7)	Relative Root Mean Square Error[b] (8)
17	Change in Business Inventories	1947–54	−0.2	3.2	3.2	.821	−0.3	3.8	3.8	.905
18		1955–61	−1.4	1.8	2.3	.719	−0.0	2.2	2.2	.595
19	Gov't. Expenditures on Goods and Services	1947–54	3.7	1.5	3.9	1.345	−0.1	1.5	1.5	.714
20		1955–61	0.3	1.3	1.4	1.167	−0.1	1.0	1.0	.909
21	Federal	1947–54	3.7	1.5	4.0	1.379	−0.1	1.4	1.4	.700
22		1955–61	0.1	1.2	1.2	1.200	−0.1	0.8	0.8	.889
23	State and Local	1947–54	0.1	0.4	0.4	1.333	−0.0	0.4	0.4	1.333
24		1955–61	0.2	0.9	0.9	2.250	−0.1	0.4	0.4	1.000
25	Net Exports	1947–54	−3.4	1.7	3.8	3.455	−0.2	2.3	2.2	1.833
26		1955–61	−1.8	0.7	1.9	1.900	0.1	0.6	0.6	.667

NOTE: Details in column (1) and (5) may not sum to aggregates because of rounding.

[a]See notes to Table 2 for a description of the estimates and their sources. For a description of the error statistics see Table 1, note c.

[b]Relative root mean square error is the root mean square error of the provisional estimates, M_0, divided by M_X, where $\sqrt{M_X} = \sqrt{(1-r^2)S^2_{A_n}}$, and r is the serial correlation in A_n.

The error statistics in Table 11 show that the answer to the second question is yes. A substantial decrease in the absolute errors in the provisional estimates of quarterly change is still shown between the early (1947–54 in this case) and the later (1955–61) period. For most variables, there was a reduction in the mean error as well as in the variability of the errors (columns 5 and 6).

However, there has been a much less striking decline in the errors relative to extrapolation errors ($\sqrt{M_x}$). Although the root mean square errors were smaller in eleven of the thirteen series, the relative errors declined in only six. Two of the six, however, are variables generally thought least reliable: change in business inventories and net exports.

Comparisons of quarterly level errors in the two periods give results somewhat different than those for changes. Here absolute and relative errors move together. Although errors in the levels of GNP and two major components, personal consumption expenditures and gross private domestic investment, have increased, errors in the levels of seven other series have decreased.

While there is certainly evidence of genuine improvement over time in some of the early series, it is by no means as widespread as comparisons of the absolute error statistics would suggest. The greatest improvements in accuracy have been in the data on producers' durable equipment, change in business inventories, and net exports of goods and services.

The quarterly level and change errors in GNP and its components are shown in Chart 4. The most pronounced differences between the first and second half of the period occur in total GNP. There has been an improvement in the accuracy of the quarterly change estimates, but not in quarterly levels.

The within year patterns of GNP change errors bear a striking similarity to the seasonal pattern in GNP (as shown in Chart 6 below), which would suggest that most of the improvement in GNP change estimates has come from a more accurate seasonal adjustment of the initial GNP figures.[37]

---

[37] This would be consistent with the conclusion that the producers' durables and the inventory components improved most over time. Accuracy of the anticipated plant and equipment expenditures series was greatly improved by the introduction of a seasonal adjustment. The early figures on inventory changes tended to be overadjusted until about 1957 (see Chart 6 below).

CHART 4. Errors in Provisional Estimates of Quarterly Levels and Changes in Gross National Product and Its Major Components, 1947 II–1961 IV

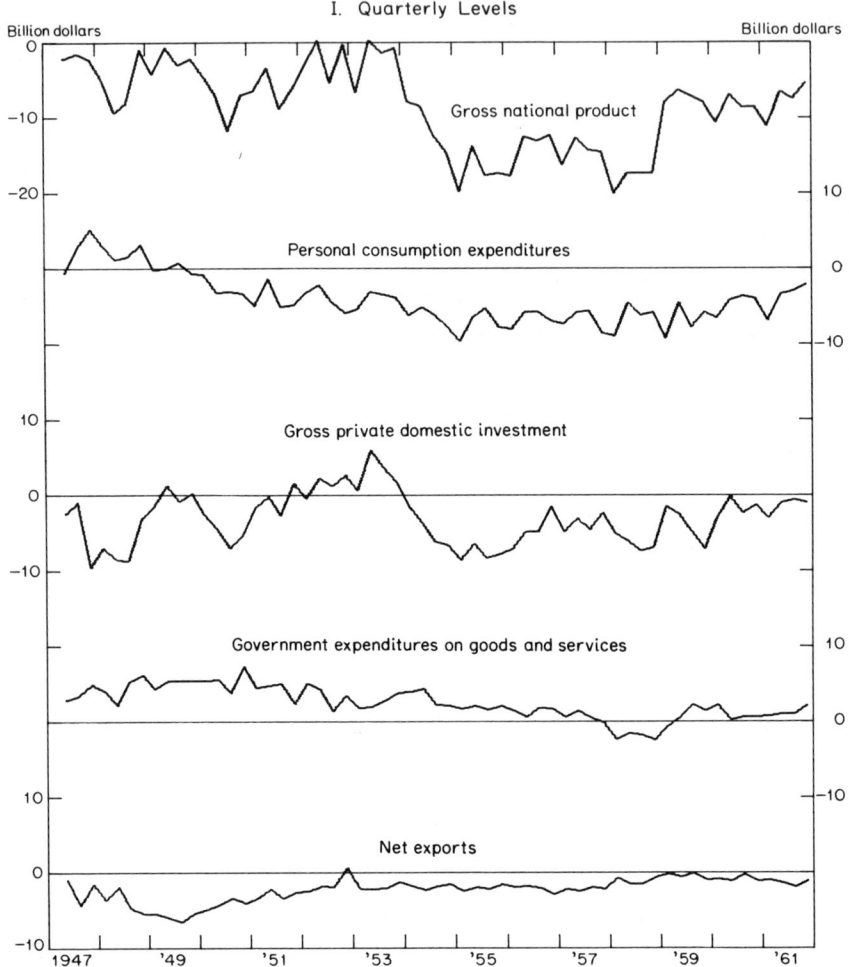

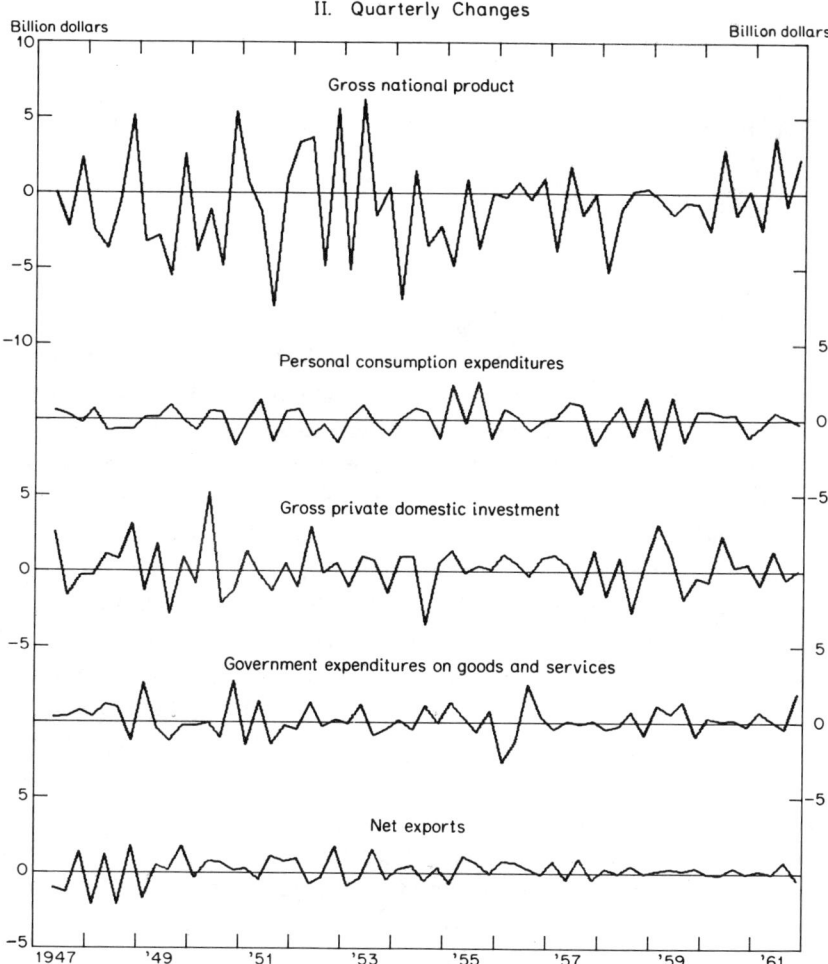

II. Quarterly Changes

V

Expenditures Estimates Compared with Income Estimates

Accuracy of Successive Estimates

One conclusion of the preceding analysis is that the provisional estimates can be viewed as relying partly on extrapolations, and that the revisions are primarily a measure of the extrapolation error. Since less extrapolation would be required for the income side of the accounts, we might then expect that the estimates of GNP derived from income data would be revised less and that they might give a better indication of the final expenditures estimates than the initial expenditures estimates do. For example, the errors of benchmark extrapolation that are included in the expenditures estimates have few counterparts in the income estimates. Moreover, there is no body of data for the expenditures estimates that is comparable to the highly reliable wage and salary component of the income estimates. On the other hand, the data for individual proprietors' income are relatively unreliable, and there are no early data on profits.

Table 12 compares the accuracy of the two sets of estimates. Not surprisingly, it shows that the income estimates are revised less than the expenditures estimates (compare lines 1 through 4 with the corresponding entries in lines 5–8).

If the income estimates (A_j^*) contained less error than the corresponding expenditures estimates (A_j), they would be better predictions of A_n. With only one exception, the estimates of quarterly levels and changes in GNP based on income (A_j^*) do show slightly greater over-all accuracy than A_j (columns 3 and 6, lines 1–4 compared with lines 9–12). They are less biased initially, though the advantage decreases as

TABLE 12. Errors in Expenditures Estimates Compared with Errors in Income Estimates of Quarterly Levels and Changes in Gross National Product, 1947 II–1961 IV (billion dollars)

Line	Code of Estimate[a]	Quarterly Levels			Quarterly Changes		
		Mean Error (1)	Standard Deviation of Error (2)	Root Mean Square Error (3)	Mean Error (4)	Standard Deviation of Error (5)	Root Mean Square Error (6)
		EXPENDITURES ESTIMATES (GNP)[b]					
1	A_0	−8.9	5.6	10.5	−0.6	3.2	3.2
2	A_1	−6.1	4.8	7.7	−0.4	2.9	2.9
3	A_2	−5.3	4.2	6.7	−0.1	2.4	2.4
4	A_3	−5.0	3.6	6.1	−0.0	2.0	2.0
		INCOME ESTIMATES					
		(GNP, exclusive of the statistical discrepancy)[c]					
5	A_0^*	−5.4	6.3	6.6	−0.3	2.2	2.2
6	A_1^*	−4.0	5.0	6.3	−0.4	1.8	1.8
7	A_2^*	−3.4	4.4	5.5	−0.3	1.4	1.4
8	A_3^*	−3.0	3.4	4.5	−0.1	1.3	1.3
		INCOME ESTIMATES AS PREDICTIONS OF					
		FINAL EXPENDITURES ESTIMATES[d]					
9	A_0^*	−6.8	6.3	9.2	−0.3	3.0	3.0
10	A_1^*	−5.4	4.9	7.3	−0.4	2.7	2.7
11	A_2^*	−4.8	4.5	6.6	−0.2	2.3	2.3
12	A_3^*	−4.4	3.8	5.8	−0.1	2.3	2.3

[a]The estimates refer to quarter t of year T.

Estimate	Date of Publication
A_0	$t + 2$ months
A_0^*	$t + 3$ months
A_1 and A_1^*	July, $T + 1$
A_2 and A_2^*	July, $T + 2$
A_3 and A_3^*	July, $T + 3$

[b]Errors are computed as $A_j - A_n$, where A_n denotes the 1965 statistically revised estimates.
[c]Errors are computed as $A_j^* - A_n^*$.
[d]Errors are computed as $A_j^* - A_n$.

the estimates are revised and in fact vanishes in the change estimates with the second July revision (columns 1 and 4). Income estimates of levels are less efficient than the expenditures estimates, but in the case of changes, they are initially more efficient (columns 2 and 5).

In sum, Table 12 suggests there is no great difference between the accuracy of the early expenditures estimates and that of the early income estimates of GNP. Any differences in the primary data which would favor the accuracy of the income estimates are apparently offset by the errors arising from the lack of early data on profits.

Use of the Statistical Discrepancy to Measure Error

Another implication of the conclusion that revisions are primarily a measure of extrapolation errors is that the revisions may give almost no indication of the magnitude or the behavior of total measurement error.[38] Indeed, extrapolation error may be a very small element of the total error ($E_0 = \epsilon + E_n$).

Some indirect evidence on total error is provided by the statistical discrepancy, the item in the national accounts which reconciles the income with the product, or expenditures, estimates. The discrepancy between the two sets of GNP estimates (D_j) can be written

$$D_j = A_j - A_j^* = E_j - E_j^* \quad (j = 0, \cdots, n),$$

where A_j stands for the product estimates, A_j^* for the income estimates, and E_j and E_j^* for their respective errors.

Under strong but not unreasonable assumptions, the discrepancy can be used in conjunction with the revisions to obtain two types of error estimates: (1) rough estimates of the fraction of error eliminated by successive revisions and (2) rough estimates of the ratio of measurement error variance to the variance of the final series.

If extrapolation errors were important components of the initial errors, E_0 and E_0^*, respectively, their elimination through successive revisions of the estimates would result in a substantial reduction in the discrepancy. The variance of the initial discrepancy (D_0) would be

$$\sigma^2(D_0) = \sigma^2(E_0 - E_0^*) = \sigma^2(\epsilon - \epsilon^*) + \sigma^2(E_n - E_n^*),$$
$$\text{assuming Cov}(\epsilon - \epsilon^*, E_n - E_n^*) = 0,$$

and the variance of the final discrepancy (D_n) would be

$$\sigma^2(D_n) = \sigma^2(E_n - E_n^*).$$

[38] However, the revisions would give a rough index of accuracy among the components of GNP if there were a positive correlation between ϵ_i and E_{ni}, the error in measuring the ith component.

We would then expect $\sigma^2(D_n) < \sigma^2(D_0)$ and, indeed, the following tabulation shows that the revisions reduced the variance of the initial discrepancy by more than half:

Statistical Discrepancy Between Estimates of GNP Based on Expenditures and Income Data, 1947 II–1961 IV

		$\sigma^2(D_j)$
Provisional Estimates	$D_0 = E_0 - E_0^*$	7.95
First July Revised Estimates	$D_1 = E_1 - E_1^*$	6.10
Second July Revised Estimates	$D_2 = E_2 - E_2^*$	4.84
Third July Revised Estimates	$D_3 = E_3 - E_3^*$	4.41
1965 Revised Estimates	$D_n = E_n - E_n^*$	3.46

It might be tempting to conclude that the revisions eliminated somewhat over one-half of the initial measurement error. However, this conclusion would be correct only under certain conditions. To illustrate what is involved, assume that:

(1) The revisions are an exact measure of extrapolation errors and that they are independent of other types of measurement errors. Then,

$$\text{Cov}(\epsilon, E_n) = \text{Cov}(\epsilon^*, E_n^*) = 0,$$

such that

$$\sigma^2(E_0) = \sigma^2(\epsilon) + \sigma^2(E_n) \text{ and } \sigma^2(E_0^*) = \sigma^2(\epsilon^*) + \sigma^2(E_n^*).$$

(2) Errors in the income and in the expenditures estimates are of the same magnitude, such that

$$\sigma^2(\epsilon) = \sigma^2(\epsilon^*) \text{ and } \sigma^2(E_0) = \sigma^2(E_n^*).$$

The ratio of the variances of the initial and the final discrepancy could then be written

$$\frac{\sigma^2(D_0)}{\sigma^2(D_n)} = \frac{2\sigma^2(\epsilon)(1 - r_{\epsilon\epsilon}^*) + 2\sigma^2(E_n)(1 - r_{E_n E_n^*})}{2\sigma^2(E_n)(1 - r_{E_n E_n^*})}$$

$$= 1 + \frac{\sigma^2(\epsilon)(1 - r_{\epsilon\epsilon}^*)}{\sigma^2(E_n)(1 - r_{E_n E_n^*})}$$

In the special case in which the correlations between the two extrapolation errors and between the two remaining errors are equal ($r_{\epsilon\epsilon}^* = r_{E_n E_n^*}$),

$$\frac{\sigma^2(D_0)}{\sigma^2(D_n)} - 1 = \frac{\sigma^2(\epsilon)}{\sigma^2(E_n)}.$$

Since $\dfrac{\sigma^2(D_0)}{\sigma^2(D_n)} = 2.298$, $\dfrac{\sigma^2(\epsilon)}{\sigma^2(E_n)} = 1.298$ and since $\sigma^2(\epsilon) = (5.6)^2 = 31.36$, $\sigma^2(E_n) = 31.36 \div 1.298 = 24.16$, then $\dfrac{\sigma^2(\epsilon)}{\sigma^2(E_0)} = \dfrac{31.36}{31.36 + 24.16} = .554$.

Thus under these special conditions, extrapolation error would amount to about 55 per cent of the initial measurement error, or put differently, the revisions eliminated about 55 per cent of the initial error.

It could be objected, however, that the reduction in the discrepancy may overstate the error eliminated by the revisions (or in other words, the importance of extrapolation error). The statistical discrepancy, as noted earlier, serves as a tool for controlling error. An unusually large discrepancy suggests the presence of unusual error in either the income or in the expenditures estimates and an attempt is generally made to trace the error and eliminate it before the figures are released. Hence the discrepancy as published is not a pure residual and the revisions, it might be contended, reflect in part an allocation of the discrepancy.

It is clear, however, that the revisions of the expenditures estimates do not *primarily* reflect an allocation of the discrepancy—or the revisions of GNP components, as well as of the aggregate, would not have resembled extrapolation errors. It is nonetheless possible that the revisions *in part* reflect an effort to bring the income and product estimates together. It would therefore be well to consider the estimate of the fraction of error eliminated by the revisions (.554) an upper limit and the estimate of the variance of E_n (24.16), a lower limit.

Alternative estimates can be obtained from the final discrepancy in the following way: Assume, as before, that the errors remaining in both sets of estimates are of the same magnitude such that

$$\sigma^2(E_n) = \sigma^2(E_n^*).$$

The variance of the final discrepancy could then be written

$$\sigma^2(D_n) = 2\sigma^2(E_n)(1 - r_{E_n E_n^*}),$$

and

$$\sigma^2(E_n) = \dfrac{\sigma^2(D_n)}{2(1 - r_{E_n E_n^*})}.$$

Estimates of $\sigma^2(E_n)$ can be computed for given values of $r_{E_n E_n^*}$. For example, if $r_{E_n E_n^*}$ were $+.9$, $\sigma^2(E_n)$ would be five times $\sigma^2(D_n)$, or, if

$r_{E_n E_n^*}$ were equal to $+.95$, $\sigma^2(E_n)$ would be ten times $\sigma^2(D_n)$. The following tabulation shows estimates of $\sigma^2(E_n)$ for arbitrary values of $r_{E_n E_n^*}$. These estimates are added to the variance of the revisions to obtain crude estimates of $\sigma^2(E_0)$, the initial error. The last two columns show the variance of the revisions as a fraction of the variance of the initial error and the initial error as a fraction of the variance of the final series.

Estimates of Error

Assumed Value of $r_{E_n E_n^*}$	$\sigma^2(E_n) = \dfrac{\sigma^2(D_n)}{2(1 - r_{E_n E_n^*})}$		$\sigma^2(E_0) = \sigma^2(\epsilon) + \sigma^2(E_n)$	$\dfrac{\sigma^2(\epsilon)}{\sigma^2(E_0)}$	$\dfrac{\sigma^2(E_0)}{\sigma^2(A_n)}$
.950	34.6		66.0	.475	.008
.975	69.2		100.6	.313	.012
.990	173.0		204.6	.153	.025
.995	346.0		377.4	.083	.045

These error estimates are of course crude and they are based on strong assumptions, which may not be fulfilled. Nonetheless they provide some indication of orders of magnitude. Taking them at face value, they would suggest that the revisions eliminated anywhere from 8 to nearly 50 per cent of the initial error and that the initial measurement error could range from roughly 1 to 5 per cent of the variance of GNP for the period covered, 1947 II–1961 IV.

VI

Revisions in Major Patterns of Change

The variance of GNP over time consists mainly of short-term cyclical and seasonal, and longer term, trend movements. This section compares the initial estimates of these major patterns of change with the successively revised estimates.[39]

Cyclical Changes

Short-term movements in GNP, computed by using the most recent estimates available at a given time, t, are subject to future revision. For example, a segment of quarterly values of GNP, observed in period t and going two years into the past,

$$A_{0_t}, A_{0_{t-1}}, A_{0_{t-2}}, A_{1_{t-3}}, A_{1_{t-4}}, A_{1_{t-5}}, A_{1_{t-6}}, A_{2_{t-7}}$$

is revised and the estimates of GNP for the same periods become

$$A_{1_t}, A_{1_{t-1}}, A_{1_{t-2}}, A_{2_{t-3}}, A_{2_{t-4}}, A_{2_{t-5}}, A_{2_{t-6}}, A_{3_{t-7}}$$

approximately one year later. As noted earlier, the initial estimate of GNP for a given period is typically revised at least five times. Thus the magnitudes of cyclical expansion or decline might appear quite different in retrospect than they would seem to a current observer watching each cyclical phase as it unfolds.

[39] Unless otherwise noted, the fully revised 1965 data are used throughout this section. (That is, the 1965 data include both statistical and definitional revisions.) This has been done mainly to simulate more accurately the patterns of change in GNP and its components as they would appear to users.

CHART 5. First and Revised Estimates of the Decline in GNP During Four Postwar Contractions and the First Year of Recovery

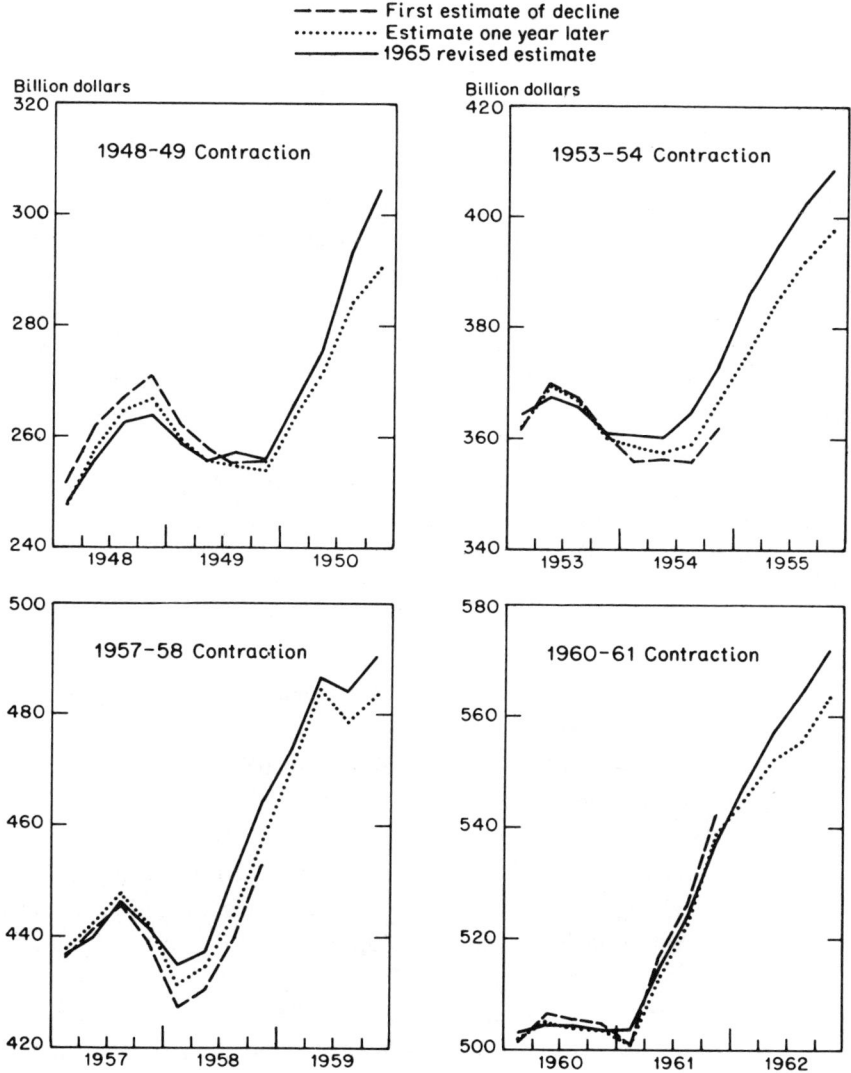

AMPLITUDES. Chart 5 compares the first and revised (1965) estimates of the path of GNP decline and of the first year of recovery for each of the four postwar contractions. Two- and three-year segments of the most recent series available at the time are shown and they are compared with the 1965 estimates of the period.

The first estimates tend to overstate levels in the vicinity of peaks and underestimate in the vicinity of troughs, although there are some exceptions. The over-all impression is one of overestimation of cyclical declines.

Estimates of the strength of the recoveries show a mixed picture. The magnitudes of the recoveries after the 1949 and 1954 troughs are underestimated, approximately correct after 1958, and slightly overstated in 1961 and then understated in 1962. The effect of the 1959 steel strike is overestimated by the first figures.

Three of the eight turning points are incorrectly dated by the first estimates (1949, 1954, and 1961); two are instances of late dating.

Table 13a shows the revisions in the magnitude of two estimates of gross national product decline from peak to trough for the four postwar contractions. As suggested by Chart 5, the magnitude of the decline in each of the four contractions has been consistently revised downward and substantially so for both estimates of GNP.

Table 13b shows the revisions in the magnitude of two estimates of GNP increase from trough to peak for three postwar expansions. The revisions are mixed: the increase during the 1949–53 expansion was revised downward, the increase during 1954–57 was revised upward, and the increase during 1958–60 was revised mainly downward.

The initial estimates tend to overestimate peak and underestimate trough levels, except for the peak in 1957 which was underestimated by both the expenditures and income estimates. The estimates of GNP based on income show somewhat less bias at troughs and peaks. Consequently, they show less bias in the initial estimates of the magnitude of cyclical decline or expansion.

The magnitudes of the 1948–49 and 1960–61 contractions appear slightly more severe when measured by the income than by the product estimates; the opposite is true for the 1953–54 and 1957–58 declines. The product estimates show the 1957–58 decline, when measured by the absolute decrease, to be the most severe, while the income estimates show the most severe decline was in 1947–49.[40] In terms of percentage decline, both estimates show 1948–49 to have been the most severe, followed by 1957–58, 1953–54, and 1960–61.

The initial overestimate of the severity of GNP decline in all four

---

[40] This is true only for the 1965 estimates. Prior to 1965, the estimates based on income also showed the 1957–58 decline as the most severe.

TABLE 13A. Revisions in Two Estimates of Peak to Trough Decline in GNP During Four Postwar Contractions, Classified by First to Latest Date Decline Measured
(billion dollars)

Date Decline Measured[a]		GROSS NATIONAL PRODUCT				GROSS NATIONAL PRODUCT, EXCLUSIVE OF STATISTICAL DISCREPANCY			
		Level at		Peak to Trough Change		Level at		Peak to Trough Change	
		Peak[b] (1)	Trough[b] (2)	Absolute (3)	Percentage (4)	Peak[b] (5)	Trough[b] (6)	Absolute (7)	Percentage (8)
		1948–49 CONTRACTION							
February	1950	270.3	255.2	−15.1	−5.6	271.1	255.7	−15.4	−5.7
July	1950	266.8	253.8	−13.0	−4.9	269.7	255.1	−14.6	−5.4
July	1951	267.0	255.5	−11.5	−4.3	269.7	255.8	−13.9	−5.2
July	1952	267.0	256.8	−10.2	−3.8	266.0	253.5	−12.5	−4.7
Major Revision	1954	264.0	255.5	−8.5	−3.2	267.1	255.5	−11.6	−4.3
Major Revision	1958	265.9	257.0	−8.9	−3.3	266.1	253.8	−12.3	−4.6
Major Revision	1965	263.9	255.0	−8.9	−3.4				
		1953–54 CONTRACTION							
August	1954	369.9	356.0	−13.9	−3.8	367.4	359.9	−7.5	−2.0
July	1955	369.3	357.6	−11.7	−3.2	363.8	355.6	−8.2	−2.2
July	1956	367.4	358.5	−8.9	−2.4	363.8	356.5	−7.3	−2.0
July	1957	367.4	358.7	−8.7	−2.4	366.8	359.7	−7.1	−1.9
Major Revision	1958	368.8	358.9	−9.9	−2.7	364.5	357.6	−6.9	−1.9
Major Revision	1965	367.5	360.4	−7.1	−1.9				
		1957–58 CONTRACTION							
May	1958	440.0	422.0	−18.0	−4.1	444.9	427.5	−17.4	−3.9
July	1958	445.6	425.8	−19.8	−4.4	447.5	432.2	−15.3	−3.4
July	1959	447.8	431.0	−16.8	−3.8	448.9	434.5	−14.4	−3.2
July	1960	448.3	432.0	−16.3	−3.6	448.9	434.8	−14.1	−3.1
July	1961	448.3	432.9	−15.4	−3.4	445.6	435.0	−10.6	−2.4
Major Revision	1965	446.3	434.7	−11.6	−2.6				
		1960–61 CONTRACTION							
May	1961	505.0	499.8	−5.2	−1.0	509.3	503.4	−5.9	−1.2
July	1961	506.4	500.8	−5.6	−1.1	509.3	503.9	−5.4	−1.1
July	1962	504.8	500.8	−4.0	−.8	508.0	503.2	−4.8	−.9
July	1963	504.1	500.4	−3.7	−.7	508.0	503.9	−4.1	−.8
July	1964	504.1	501.4	−2.7	−.5	507.4	502.2[c]	−5.2[c]	−1.0[c]
Major Revision	1965	504.7	503.3[c]	−1.4[c]	−.3[c]				

NOTE: Footnotes follow Table 13b.

TABLE 13B. Revisions in Two Estimates of Trough to Peak Increase in GNP During Three Postwar Expansions Classified by First to Latest Date Increase Measured
(billion dollars)

Date Increase Measured[a]		GROSS NATIONAL PRODUCT				GROSS NATIONAL PRODUCT, EXCLUSIVE OF STATISTICAL DISCREPANCY			
		Level at		Trough to Peak Change		Level at		Trough to Peak Change	
		Trough[b] (1)	Peak[b] (2)	Absolute (3)	Percentage (4)	Trough[b] (5)	Peak[b] (6)	Absolute (7)	Percentage (8)
1949–53 EXPANSION									
August	1953	256.8	372.4	115.6	45.0				
Major Revision	1954	255.5	369.9	114.4	44.8	253.5	367.3	113.8	44.9
July	1955	255.5	369.3	113.8	44.5	253.5	367.4	113.9	44.9
July	1956	255.5	367.4	111.9	43.8	253.5	363.8	110.3	43.5
Major Revision	1958	257.0	368.8	111.8	43.5	255.5	366.8	111.3	43.6
1954–57 EXPANSION									
November	1957	358.7	439.0	80.3	22.4	356.5	436.5	80.0	22.4
Major Revision	1958	358.9	445.6	86.7	24.2	359.7	444.9	85.2	23.7
July	1959	358.9	447.8	88.9	24.8	359.7	447.5	87.8	24.4
July	1960	358.9	448.3	89.4	24.9	359.7	448.9	89.2	24.8
Major Revision	1965	360.4	446.3	85.9	23.8	357.6	445.6	88.0	24.6
1958–60 EXPANSION									
August	1960	432.0	505.0	73.0	16.9				
July	1961	432.9	506.4	73.5	17.0	434.8	509.3	74.5	17.1
July	1962	432.9	504.8	71.9	16.6	434.8	509.3	74.5	17.1
July	1963	432.9	504.1	71.2	16.4	434.8	508.0	73.2	16.8
Major Revision	1965	434.7	504.7	70.0	16.1	435.0	507.4	72.4	16.6

[a]Dates refer to the SCB issue in which the level estimates are published. Major revisions of the estimates are from SCB supplements: *National Income* (1954 revision) and *U.S. Income and Output* (1958 revision). The 1965 revision is taken from the August 1965 SCB.

[b]The peak and trough dates used are specific cycle dates for GNP. They are:

Contraction	Peak	Trough
1947–49	IV 1948	IV 1949
1953–54	II 1953	II 1954
1957–58	III 1957	I 1958
1960–61	II 1960	I 1961

One exception to the use of these dates is noted in footnote c below.
[c]The major revision of 1965 changed the date of the trough from 1961 I to 1960 IV. The figures refer to a 1960 IV trough.

postwar contractions was the consequence of underestimating the rise in personal consumption expenditudes and overestimating the decline in gross private domestic investment. The revisions in the initial estimates of peak to trough change in the major components of GNP are shown in Table 14a.

There was an initial overestimate of the decline or underestimate of the rise in consumption expenditures on goods during all four contractions. The rise in expenditures on services tended to be underestimated only in 1953–54 and 1957–58.

The decrease in the change in business inventories was consistently and substantially overstated by the early estimates. The decreases in expenditures on producers' durable equipment were initially underestimated except in 1953–54 and 1960–61. There appears to have been little systematic bias in the initial estimates of change in new construction expenditures.

Changes in federal government expenditures on goods and services tended to be overestimated except in 1957–58. The rise in state and local government expenditures was underestimated except during 1960–61.

Revisions of the first estimates of trough to peak change in the major components of GNP are shown in Table 14b. The overestimates of the change in gross private domestic investment, particularly the change in business inventories, were mainly responsible for the initial overestimates of GNP change during the expansions of 1949–53 and 1958–60. The expansion of 1954–57 was underestimated by the first estimates of all the components except two: consumption expenditures on nondurables and state and local government expenditures on goods and services.

Although most of the components have contributed to the bias in the initial estimates of GNP change during periods of business cycle expansion and contraction, the role of the inventories component has been predominant. It is well known that change in business inventories is one of the weaker components in terms of accuracy, but the consequences of its measurement errors for this use of GNP statistics are perhaps less known.

TURNING-POINT DATES. Table 15 shows the effect revisions have had on the timing of major turns in GNP. Although the timing of peaks

TABLE 14A. Revisions in Estimates of Peak to Trough Changes in Major Components of GNP During Four Postwar Contractions, Classified by First to Latest Date Change Measured (billion dollars)

		ESTIMATES OF PEAK TO TROUGH CHANGES IN MAJOR COMPONENTS[b]						
		Personal Consumption Expenditures				Gross Private Domestic Investment		
Date Change Measured[a]		Total (1)	Nondurables (2)	Durables (3)	Services (4)	Total (5)	Change in Business Inventories (6)	Producers' Durable Equipment (7)	New Construction (8)

Date Change Measured[a]		Total (1)	Nondurables (2)	Durables (3)	Services (4)	Total (5)	Change in Business Inventories (6)	Producers' Durable Equipment (7)	New Construction (8)
				1948–49 CONTRACTION					
February	1950	−1.1	−5.6	2.3	2.1	−14.3	−12.7	−2.5	.8
July	1950	1.9	−3.5	3.1	2.2	−15.6	−13.7	−2.2	.4
July	1951	2.5	−3.1	2.6	3.0	−15.2	−13.3	−2.4	.4
July	1952	3.2	−2.3	2.5	3.0	−14.7	−12.6	−2.5	.4
Major Revision	1954	3.4	−2.8	2.8	3.3	−13.3	−11.2	−2.6	.6
Major Revision	1958	3.2	−2.9	3.2	3.0	−13.3	−9.6	−4.1	.5
Major Revision	1965	2.2	−2.9	3.2	2.0	−12.5	−9.6	−3.1	.1
				1953–54 CONTRACTION					
August	1954	2.3	.4	−1.5	3.4	−10.3	−9.2	−2.2	1.1
July	1955	3.7	.7	−1.6	4.6	−8.1	−7.2	−2.2	1.1
July	1956	3.6	.5	−1.4	4.5	−5.3	−4.8	−1.6	1.1
July	1957	3.6	.3	−1.4	4.8	−5.2	−4.6	−1.6	.9
Major Revision	1958	3.2	.2	−1.2	4.3	−5.7	−5.8	−1.1	1.1
Major Revision	1965	4.5	.2	−1.0	5.1	−5.7	−5.9	−.9	1.1
				1957–58 CONTRACTION					
May	1958	−2.4	−1.0	−3.5	2.1	−14.7	−12.0	−3.0	.3
Major Revision	1958	−2.1	−.7	−4.1	2.7	−17.1	−11.7	−5.1	−.3
July	1959	−.9	−.2	−4.0	3.4	−15.5	−9.6	−5.2	−.7
July	1960	−1.0	−.2	−4.4	3.5	−15.2	−9.4	−4.8	−1.0
July	1961	−1.3	−1.2	−4.4	3.4	−13.7	−8.0	−4.8	−.9
Major Revision	1965	.7	.1	−2.7	3.3	−13.1	−8.6	−3.4	−1.1
				1960–61 CONTRACTION					
May	1961	−.2	−.5	−4.3	5.7	−14.5	−9.8	−3.0	−1.7
July	1961	.8	.4	−5.9	6.3	−14.8	−9.4	−4.4	−1.1
July	1962	.6	.9	−5.0	4.7	−13.4	−8.0	−4.0	−1.4
July	1963	1.0	.9	−4.5	4.6	−13.7	−8.5	−3.8	−1.4
Major Revision	1965	1.4[c]	.5[c]	−2.3[c]	3.3[c]	−8.4[c]	−6.3[c]	−1.4[c]	−.7[c]

TABLE 14A. (concluded)

ESTIMATES OF PEAK TO TROUGH CHANGES IN MAJOR COMPONENTS[b]

Date Change Measured[a]		Gov't Expenditures on Goods and Services			Net Exports
		Total (9)	Federal (10)	State and Local (11)	Total (12)
1948–49 CONTRACTION					
February	1950	3.4	1.6	1.9	−3.0
July	1950	2.5	.7	1.8	−1.7
July	1951	3.0	.9	2.1	−1.7
July	1952	3.0	.9	2.1	−1.7
Major Revision	1954	3.2	1.1	2.1	−1.8
Major Revision	1958	2.1[d]	−.5[d]	2.6	−.9[d]
Major Revision	1965	3.0	.6	2.4	−1.7
1953–54 CONTRACTION					
August	1954	−8.3	−10.9	2.6	2.3
July	1955	−9.5	−12.4	3.0	2.2
July	1956	−10.0	−13.0	3.0	2.8
July	1957	−9.9	−12.9	3.0	2.8
Major Revision	1958	−8.9[d]	−11.8[d]	3.0	1.5[d]
Major Revision	1965	−7.6	−10.4	2.9	1.6
1957–58 CONTRACTION					
May	1958	1.0	−1.1	1.9	−1.7
Major Revision	1958	3.7	1.2	2.5	−3.1
July	1959	3.3	.4	2.3	−3.1
July	1960	3.2	.6	2.6	−3.4
July	1961	2.9	.6	2.3	−3.4
Major Revision	1965	3.6	.6	2.0	−2.9
1960–61 CONTRACTION					
May	1961	6.1	3.0	3.1	3.3
July	1961	5.4	1.8	3.5	3.0
July	1962	5.8	2.3	3.5	2.9
July	1963	5.8	2.5	3.3	3.1
Major Revision	1965	3.1[e]	1.6[e]	1.4[e]	2.6[e]

NOTE: Footnotes follow Table 14b.

TABLE 14B. Revisions in Estimates of Trough to Peak Changes in Major Components of GNP During Three Postwar Expansions, Classified by First to Latest Date Change Measured
(billion dollars)

		ESTIMATES OF TROUGH TO PEAK CHANGES IN MAJOR COMPONENTS[b]						
		Personal Consumption Expenditures				Gross Private Domestic Investment		
Date Change Measured[a]		Total (1)	Nondurables (2)	Durables (3)	Services (4)	Total (5)	Change in Business Inventories (6)	Producers' Durable Equipment (7)	New Construction (8)

Date Change Measured[a]		Total (1)	Nondurables (2)	Durables (3)	Services (4)	Total (5)	Change in Business Inventories (6)	Producers' Durable Equipment (7)	New Construction (8)
		1949–53 EXPANSION							
August	1954	47.4	23.0	5.7	18.7	30.0	14.2	8.7	7.1
Major Revision	1954	47.3	23.0	5.2	19.2	26.8	11.7	7.7	7.3
July	1955	47.9	23.1	5.5	19.4	25.9	10.8	7.5	7.6
July	1956	47.9	23.2	5.5	19.3	24.4	9.4	7.3	7.6
Major Revision	1958	49.3	22.3	7.1	19.7	22.3	8.4	6.0	7.9
Major Revision	1965	51.3	23.2	7.2	21.0	21.6	8.5	5.6	7.6
		1954–57 EXPANSION							
November	1957	48.6	22.4	5.8	20.3	17.2	3.5	7.9	5.9
Major Revision	1958	51.8	21.7	8.2	21.9	19.5	4.9	7.1	7.7
July	1959	51.7	20.9	8.7	22.1	20.7	5.4	8.1	7.3
July	1960	52.2	20.9	8.7	22.5	20.4	5.2	8.0	7.3
Major Revision	1965	49.2	20.3	8.1	21.0	20.7	5.9	8.7	6.1
		1958–60 EXPANSION							
August	1960	41.3	13.8	8.0	19.4	23.1	12.2	5.4	5.5
July	1961	42.5	13.8	8.8	19.8	20.7	10.9	4.5	5.4
July	1962	42.5	13.1	9.3	20.1	19.6	9.9	4.3	5.4
July	1963	42.3	13.5	9.2	19.6	19.4	9.7	4.3	5.4
Major Revision	1965	41.8	14.2	8.2	19.2	18.7	9.3	5.5	3.9

TABLE 14B. (concluded)

ESTIMATES OF TROUGH TO PEAK CHANGES IN MAJOR COMPONENTS[b]

Date Change Measured[a]		Gov't. Expenditures on Goods and Services			Net Exports
		Total (9)	Federal (10)	State and Local (11)	Total (12)
1949–53 EXPANSION					
August	1954	40.2	34.4	5.8	−2.0
Major Revision	1954	43.2	37.7	5.5	−2.8
July	1955	42.0	36.5	5.4	−2.0
July	1956	42.1	36.7	5.4	−2.5
Major Revision	1958	43.0[c]	37.3[c]	5.6	−2.8[c]
Major Revision	1965	43.3	37.7	5.6	−3.7
1954–57 EXPANSION					
November	1957	11.1	2.3	8.8	3.4
Major Revision	1958	11.4[c]	2.6[c]	8.8	4.0[c]
July	1959	12.2	2.6	9.6	4.3
July	1960	12.5	2.9	9.6	4.3
Major Revision	1965	12.3	2.3	9.9	3.8
1958–60 EXPANSION					
August	1960	8.5	1.1	7.4	.3
July	1961	9.8	2.3	7.6	.6
July	1962	9.2	2.5	6.7	.7
July	1963	9.1	2.3	6.8	.6
Major Revision	1965	8.6	1.7	7.0	.9

[a]See note a to Tables 13a and 13b for source of data.
[b]See note b to Tables 13a and 13b for peak and trough dates used.
[c]The figures refer to a 1960 IV trough.
[d]Figures are not comparable to preceding figures in the column because of a definitional change. The major revision of 1958 changed the treatment of federal government international transfer payments. Cash grants to foreign countries are no longer a component of GNP (i.e., no longer included in federal government purchases of goods and services and deducted from exports of goods and services).

TABLE 15. Revisions of Major Turning Point Dates in Two Estimates of Gross National Product

Date of Publication and Source[b]	Dates of Peaks		Date of Publication and Source[b]	Dates of Troughs[a]	
	GNP	GNP, Exclusive of Statistical Discrepancy		GNP	GNP, Exclusive of Statistical Discrepancy
I. *1948–49 Contraction*					
May 1949 (*SCB*)	1948 IV		January 1950 (*ERP*)	(1949 IV)	
August 1949 through			February 1950 (*SCB*)	1949 III	
August 1965 (*SCB*)		1948 IV	May 1950 (*SCB*)	1949 III	(1949 IV)
			July 1950 through		
			August 1965 (*SCB*)	1949 IV	1949 IV
II. *1953–54 Contraction*					
October 1953 (*EI*)	1953 II		July 1954 (*EI*)	(1954 II)	
February 1954 through			August 1954 (*SCB*) through		
August 1965 (*SCB*)		1953 II	October 1954 (*EI*)	1954 I	
			November 1954 (*SCB*)	(1954 III)	1954 I
			January 1955 (*ERP*) through		
			May 1955 (*SCB*)	1954 III	1954 I
			July 1955 (*SCB*)	1954 II	1954 I
			July 1956 through		
			July 1957 (*SCB*)	1953 IV	1953 IV
			July 1958 (*SCB*)	1954 II	1954 I
			August 1965 (*SCB*)	1954 II	1953 IV

TABLE 15. (concluded)

	Dates of Peaks		Dates of Troughs[a]	
Date of Publication and Source[b]	GNP	GNP, Exclusive of Statistical Discrepancy	Date of Publication and Source[b]	GNP	GNP, Exclusive of Statistical Discrepancy

Date of Publication and Source[b]	GNP	GNP, Exclusive of Statistical Discrepancy	Date of Publication and Source[b]	GNP	GNP, Exclusive of Statistical Discrepancy
III. *1957–58 Contraction*					
January 1958 (*ERP*) through August 1965 (*SCB*)	1957 III		July 1958 through August 1965 (*SCB*)	1958 I	
February 1958 through August 1965 (*SCB*)		1957 III	October 1958 (*EI*) through August 1965 (*SCB*)		1958 I
IV. *1960–61 Contraction*					
October 1960 (*EI*) through August 1965 (*SCB*)	1960 II		July 1961 (*EI*) through July 1963 (*SCB*)	1961 I	
December 1960 (*EI*) through May 1961 (*EI*)		1960 III	October 1961 (*EI*) through July 1964 (*SCB*)		1961 I
July 1961 (*EI*) through August 1965 (*SCB*)		1960 II	August 1965 (*SCB*)	1960 IV	1960 IV

[a]Dates in parentheses indicate the given quarter was lower than the preceding quarter. Since data for the succeeding quarter were not available, the designation of a trough is uncertain.

[b]SCB stands for *Survey of Current Business*, EI for *Economic Indicators*, and ERP for the *Economic Report of the President*.

was unaffected, the dates of the low points in three of the four cyclical declines in GNP were changed. Only the date of the trough in 1958 appears the same throughout the early and successively revised figures.

As Chart 5 shows, however, the troughs of the declines beginning in 1948, 1953, and 1960 are not marked by a single quarter, or turning point, but rather by a leveling off period, or turning zone. In these cases, even small revisions in the estimates are sufficient to change the low point by one or even two quarters. The flat trough of the 1953–54 contraction is the most pronounced and, as Table 15 shows, the low point of this decline differs by as much as three quarters in the product data and by one quarter in the income data.

Now and then the suggestion comes up that a chronology of business cycles ought to be based on the cyclical timing of a single measure of aggregate economic activity: for example, gross national product or industrial production. The frequent revisions of GNP, and the differences between the income and expenditure estimates, are two of the difficulties associated with relying exclusively on the timing of GNP to date business cycles.[41]

Revisions are by no means limited to gross national product statistics. Stekler's study shows that the dates of major turning points in the Federal Reserve Board's Index of Industrial Production have undergone considerable revision as a result of both changes in weights and methods of reporting.[42] Unlike the revisions of GNP which have mainly affected troughs, revisions in the production index have primarily changed peaks. Moreover, the differences in timing are fairly large. For example, the 1948 peak in production first appeared to be in November, then in August, and later in July. Similarly, the 1953 peak is first shown in March, but the revised data show it in July. The dates of other major turns in industrial production were altered by no more than one month.

The foregoing discussion has shown some of the difficulties that errors in the early GNP statistics create for those who would use movements in GNP as an indicator of current business conditions. Most

---

[41] For a discussion of the problems, see Victor Zarnowitz, "On The Dating of Business Cycles," *Journal of Business,* April 1963, pp. 197–199. This article is a reply to George W. Cloos, "How Good Are The National Bureau's Reference Dates?," *Journal of Business,* January 1963. The exchange is continued in the July and October issues of the same journal.

[42] Stekler, *op. cit.,* Table 8.

serious for policy makers are the misleading ideas of magnitude that may be engendered by the first estimates of cyclical decline in GNP and of the strength of the early recovery.

Revisions of Seasonal Factors

Part of the revision in estimates of quarterly GNP is due to revision of the factors used to adjust the estimates for seasonal variation. The accuracy of the seasonal adjustment is especially important in those series regularly consulted by students of business cycles. In the case of GNP, as Moore points out,[43]

> Sometimes the seasonal change is many times larger than the nonseasonal. . . . When this happens at a crucial turn in the business situation, the precise magnitude of the seasonal adjustment is of very great importance. For example, between the third and fourth quarters of 1948 seasonally adjusted GNP rose by $2 billion, then in the next quarter it fell $4 billion, marking the beginning of the 1949 recession. But the seasonal adjustment had eliminated a rise of nearly $15 billion between the third and fourth quarters and a decline of $21 billion between the fourth quarter and the first. . . . A year later there were equally dramatic changes marking the revival.

Estimating the seasonal movements in current data and adjusting these data to exclude seasonal variation is an example of a particular type of forecasting. Up-to-date seasonally adjusted series require forecasts of the magnitude of the seasonal component of current change in the level of the variable. Such forecasts usually depend on the periodic and recurrent nature of seasonals; that is to say they are based entirely on the variable's historical performance.

More accurate estimates of the seasonal factors for each of a given year's four quarters can be obtained once data covering the full year are in. These factors take the place of the forecast factors when the provisional estimates of GNP are revised in July following their initial publication.

The OBE's indirect method of adjusting GNP for seasonal variation

---

[43] Geoffrey H. Moore, "Seasonal Adjustment of the Income and Product Series," *A Critique of the U. S. Income and Product Accounts,* Studies in Income and Wealth, Vol. 22, Princeton University Press for the National Bureau of Economic Research, 1958, pp. 551–552.

is cause for further revision of the seasonal factors. Seasonally adjusted GNP is obtained by summing the seasonally adjusted components. As more reliable data become available, some components are revised. Often these data have slightly different seasonals and, once they are incorporated into the estimates, slightly alter the implicit seasonal factors of GNP.[44]

Revisions in the seasonal factors were mainly responsible for the changes in the dates of the 1949, 1954, and 1961 troughs. This can be demonstrated by using the August 1965 quarterly seasonal factors to adjust the earlier sets of GNP estimates.[45] When the implicit seasonal factors for 1949, estimated in 1965, are used to adjust the first and revised product estimates, a fourth quarter 1949 trough would appear in the first throughout the revised estimates (Table 15).

Similarly, when the implicit seasonals for 1953–54, estimated in August 1965, are used to adjust the initial and revised estimates, a second quarter 1954 trough would appear throughout each set of estimates of the period (Table 15). However, the 1953–54 product estimates which were revised in July 1955–57 would show a double bottom with troughs also occurring in the fourth quarter of 1953. Finally, when the 1965 factors are used to adjust each set of estimates, the low point of the decline beginning in 1960 appears without exception in the fourth quarter of 1960.

The source of some of these differences could perhaps be traced to the OBE's indirect method of adjusting GNP for seasonal variation. While this procedure has the desirable property of having the adjusted components add to the adjusted total, it may also have the undesirable property of giving the seasonal factors of volatile components, which are likely to be affected substantially by irregular movements, too great an influence on the seasonal factors derived for GNP.

One such volatile component is the change in business inventories and it exerts a strong influence on the seasonal pattern of GNP. As Chart 6 shows, the seasonal pattern in inventories (Panel 2) is exactly

[44] The OBE does not publish a series of implicit GNP seasonal factors. Both adjusted and original quarterly data are published, however, and it is possible to derive the implicit seasonals. Multiplicative factors (i.e., ratios of original to adjusted estimates) were used in the experiments reported in the text below.

[45] Although unadjusted quarterly data were not published along with the adjusted data in the OBE's preliminary report article on the 1965 major revision (*op. cit.*), the OBE kindly furnished these data.

CHART 6. First and Revised Estimates of the Implicit Seasonal Factors for Gross National Product, Change in Business Inventories, and Total Final Purchases, 1947–63

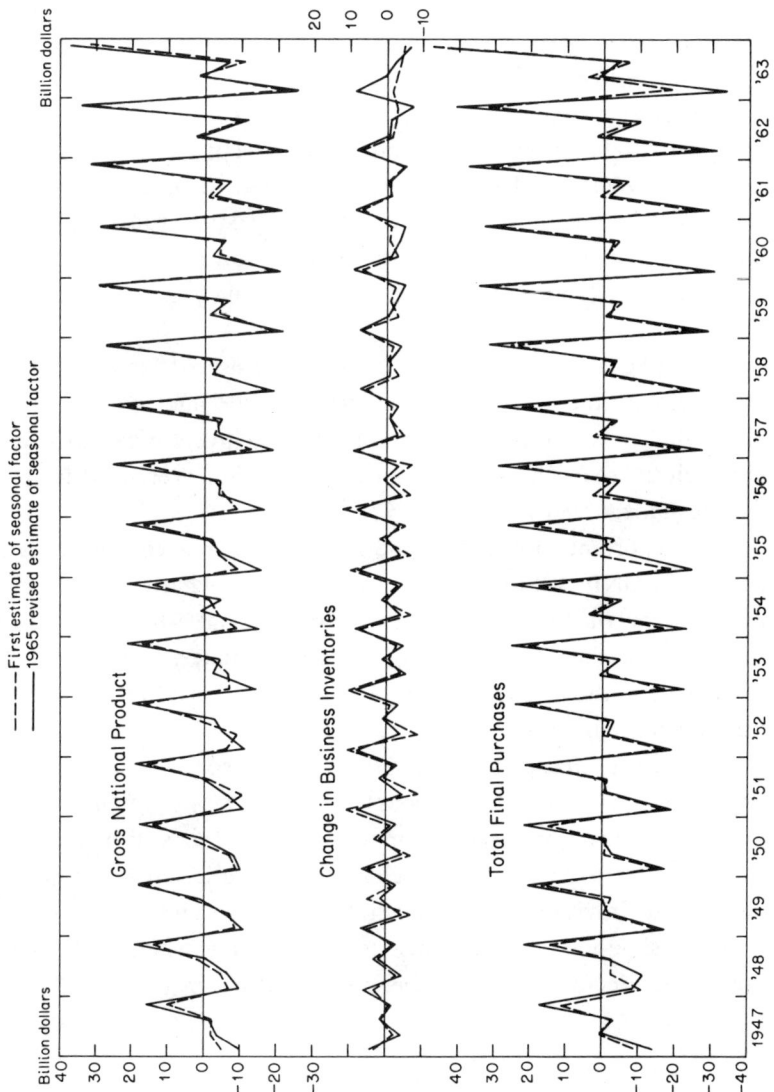

the opposite of the seasonal pattern of total final purchases (Panel 3).[46] The seasonal pattern of total final purchases increases moderately from the first to the second quarter, declines slightly from the second to the third, increases sharply from the third to the fourth, and decreases very sharply from the fourth to the first quarter of the next year.

The seasonal pattern of GNP is the net result of these two opposite patterns. It reflects mainly final purchases except for the second to third quarter movement. The pattern of the second to third quarter seasonal movement in GNP has changed over the years. From 1947 to 1952, there was a moderate rise from the second to the third quarter, a very slight decrease from 1952–57, and an increasingly greater decrease since 1958.

As can be seen from Chart 6, the initial seasonal factors have tended to understate the seasonal amplitudes in GNP and in final purchases. The initial factors for the change in business inventories show less bias, although the seasonal amplitudes were somewhat overstated from 1950–56 and understated from 1956–63.

It is important to note that the revisions do not change the seasonal pattern in GNP. Although it has changed somewhat over the years, for a given year, the pattern shown in the provisional estimates is essentially the same one that is shown in the revised estimates. From a broad point of view then, the forecasts of the seasonal component of current changes have been accurate ones.

But accurate forecasts of the seasonal *patterns* are not sufficient. For any series in which the seasonal movements are often considerably larger than the nonseasonal, small errors in the seasonal factors are enough to alter the direction of change in the adjusted series. In the case of GNP, the revisions clearly illustrate that, at certain crucial times in the business situation, an economist may not know whether the series increased or decreased during the previous quarter.

Postwar Trends

Throughout the postwar period 1947–63, the movements in gross national product show a strong upward trend with cyclical fluctuations

---

[46] The seasonal pattern in inventories can alternatively be viewed as similar to, but lagging the seasonal pattern in, final purchases by one quarter.

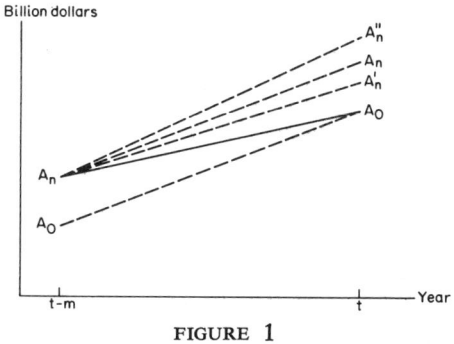

FIGURE 1

about the trend. The rate of increase, however, has not been steady; the rise was stronger during the first than during the second half of the period.

Before turning to a comparison of the first and revised average rates of increase in GNP, let us consider how they might be expected to differ. It is often suggested the revisions merely raise the level of the estimates; that they have no systematic effect on the changes. In other words, the revisions might be considered simply the sum of a constant and a random term whose expected value is zero. This is not quite the case for GNP revisions. Although the revisions raise the level of the estimates on the average, we have seen that part of the variation about the mean revision is systematic: it is partly cyclical and partly seasonal.[47]

Suppose, however, the revisions do not affect the longer term movement such that the trend in GNP over m years is the same from one set of estimates to another. Figure 1 above illustrates this special case. After n revisions, the difference between the provisional and revised estimates $(A_0 - A_n)$ is a constant and the change in the provisional estimates from year $T - m$ to T $(A_{0_T} - A_{0_{T-m}})$ is the same as the change in the revised estimates $(A_{n_T} - A_{n_{T-m}})$. But these are not the changes that an observer, standing in year T and reviewing the rise in GNP over the past m years, would note. He could not of course look at the slope of the segment $A_n A_n$—the value of A_n in year T would not be available until several years later. Typically he would look at the slope of $A_n A_0$ rather than $A_0 A_0$, which is to say he would use the series of most recent estimates available

[47] See, for example, Charts 5 and 6 and Table 3.

in year T. This series, as we have noted, is a mix of $A_0, A_1, \cdots, A_n$. Given that the revisions raise the level of the estimates, changes over several years computed from these mixed vintage data will always underestimate the increase.

It is impossible to determine a priori whether changes computed from the set of provisional estimates would overestimate or underestimate the changes computed from fully revised data and, therefore, whether or not they would be more accurate than changes computed from mixed data. They would of course exceed the rises shown by the data of mixed vintage, as long as the revisions raise the level of the estimates. For the special case in which the revisions raise the estimates by a constant amount (from A_0 to A_n in Figure 1), the provisional estimates would correctly state the rise (i.e., the slope of A_0A_0 is exactly the same as the slope of A_nA_n). If the magnitude of the revisions tends to increase over the years (e.g., in Figure 1, the revision in year $T - m$ is A_0 to A_n and from A_0 to A_n'' in year T), the provisional estimates would be underestimates. The opposite would be true if the size of the revisions tended to decrease (from A_0 to A_n in year $T - m$ to A_0 to A_n' in year t).[48]

These are somewhat surprising results. An increase in the magnitude of the revisions would suggest a deterioration over the years in the accuracy of the provisional estimates. Nonetheless, changes computed from this set of estimates would more closely resemble the changes in the fully revised figures than would the changes computed from the series of most recently available estimates. Only if the revisions show a decrease over time would changes computed from the most recent data be likely to be as accurate as the changes computed from provisional estimates. Even then, the changes based on mixed vintage data would underestimate the rise.

The extent of underestimation (or possibly overestimation on the part of the provisional estimates) depends on the magnitude of the revisions and the period of time the change covers. The average annual rates of change given in Table 16 suggest that, although the amount of underestimation is very small, there is a persistent bias in the changes computed from the most recent series available (i.e., mixed vintage data). In every case these rates of change are less than those shown by

[48]The slope of A_0A_0 exceeds that of A_nA_n' indicating the provisional estimates would overstate the rise. In the opposite case, the slope of A_0A_0 is less than that of A_nA_n''.

TABLE 16. First Compared with Revised Average Annual Rates of Increase in Two Estimates of GNP: 1947–63 and Subperiods

Line	Set of Estimates Used[a]	Average Annual Rate of Increase During:		
		1947–55 (1)	1955–63 (2) (per cent)	1947–63 (3)
	GROSS NATIONAL PRODUCT			
1	Major revision 1965	7.02	5.03	6.05
2	Major revision (statistical) 1965	7.11	5.10	6.10
3	Most recent available in Feb. 1964	6.83	4.95	5.95
4	Most recent available in Feb. 1956	6.60	—	—
5	Provisional	6.75	5.29	6.02
	GROSS NATIONAL PRODUCT, EXCLUSIVE OF THE STATISTICAL DISCREPANCY			
6	Major revision 1965	7.00	5.11	6.05
7	Major revision (statistical) 1965	7.09	5.19	6.14
8	Most recent available in Feb. 1964	6.79	5.01	5.98
9	Most recent available in Feb. 1956	6.59	—	—
10	Provisional	6.55	5.36	5.94

[a]Estimates are taken from the *Survey of Current Business*. Figures for the 1965 major revision are from the August 1965 issue. Statistical revisions are from an unpublished tabulation furnished by the OBE. The provisional estimates are from the February issues of the *Survey* of the relevant year (for example, the estimate of 1947 is from the February 1948 *Survey*).

the 1965 revised data (lines 3 and 4 compared to lines 1 and 2 and lines 8 and 9 compared to lines 6 and 7).[49]

One of the striking features of the figures in Table 16 is the very small difference in the average rates of change for a given period. There is but the slightest difference between the rates computed from the first and from the most recent figures. Thus fairly large differences in the revisions of levels create only small differences in estimates of average rates of change over several years.[50] For the estimates of GNP based on

[49] Average rates of change, depending as they do on only the base and final figures, are sensitive to unusual values. For this reason annual data are used in Table 16 and the periods are chosen to minimize as much as possible the cyclical differences among them. The years 1947, 1955, and 1963 were each rather good business years.

[50] The 1965 statistical revisions raised the level of the provisional estimates of GNP in 1947, 1955, and 1963 by 3.3, 16.2, and 15.8 billions, respectively. The

income, however, the rates computed with provisional data underestimate the rates computed with mixed vintage data during the 1947–55 and 1947–63 periods. This is unusual and it is because subsequent revisions lowered rather than raised the provisional estimates of the value of GNP in 1947.

Without exception, the different sets of data show that the increase in GNP during the second half of the period was at a lower rate than during the first half (column 2 compared to column 1). Because trend estimates based on the most recent series available tend to underestimate, one might have expected the major revision of 1965 to reduce the differential between the rates of increase in 1947–55 and 1955–63. Instead, it appears this differential has been widened in the course of revising the estimates. It is smallest in the rates computed from the provisional estimates and steadily increased in the revised data.[51]

Table 17 shows the average rates of increase during 1947–55 and 1955–63 in three major GNP components. The early figures underestimate the rates of increase in consumption expenditures during both periods and in government expenditures during 1947–55. The rate of growth in gross private domestic investment is overestimated in both periods.

All three components show a decline in the rate of increase during the second half of the postwar period. The slowdown is most pronounced in gross private domestic investment and in government expenditures.

To sum up, the initial estimates underestimate when compared with revised estimates of long-term movements in GNP during 1947–63. The main source of this underestimation is in the personal consumption expenditures. Long-term changes in gross private domestic investment are

total revisions (statistical plus definitional) are smaller, namely, 1.7, 10.8, and 4.1 billions. Note from these figures (and from Chart 4) that the magnitude of the revisions does not show a steady trend over the 1947–63 period. However, since the 1963 figure is subject to future revision, the revisions given above (15.8 and 4.1 billions) are not strictly comparable to those of the 1947 and 1955 figures. The 1965 major revision was strictly speaking only a second annual July revision of the estimates of GNP in 1963.

[51] Because revisions have generally been upward, it is reasonable to expect that subsequent revisions will raise the value of GNP in 1963, thus increasing the average rate of change from 1955–63. That is, the increase in the differential may be an illusion. It is unlikely that the differential would vanish—assuming that the figure for 1955 is correct, the level of GNP in 1963 would have to be revised upward by $100 billion to eliminate the difference in the rate of increase between 1947–55 and 1955–63.

TABLE 17. First Compared with Revised Average Annual Rates of Increase in Three Major GNP Components: 1947–55 and 1955–63

				Average Annual Rate of Change Using:[a]			
			Provisional Estimates (1)	Most Recent Series Available		1965 Major Revision	
				Feb. 1956 (2)	Feb. 1964 (3)	Total[c] (4)	Statistical (5)
Line	Major GNP Component[b]	Period Covered		(per cent)			
1	Personal Consumption Expenditures	1947–55	5.50	5.45	5.66	5.91	6.04
2	Personal Consumption Expenditures	1955–63	4.66		4.42	4.93	5.07
3	Gross Private Domestic Investment	1947–55	9.98	9.07	9.29	8.93	9.20
4	Gross Private Domestic Investment	1955–63	4.14		3.25	3.23	3.39
5	Government Expenditures	1947–55	12.93	12.97	12.87	14.58	13.37
6	Government Expenditures	1955–63	6.43		6.49	6.48	6.08

[a]See note a, Table 16, for sources of data.
[b]Net exports excluded because of negative values.
[c]Total revised estimates (statistical plus definitional revisions).

overestimated by the early figures. The rate of change in government expenditures was slightly underestimated during 1947–55 while, during 1955–63, it was slightly overestimated.

Underestimation of the aggregate's change comes about from two simple facts: GNP levels are revised upward on the average; and, at a given point in time, estimates of the most recent levels have not been revised as much as the estimates of past levels. Most users of GNP data prefer to use the series of best estimates available even though it is in fact the series containing the greatest differences over time in the accuracy (or vintage) of the estimates. If the magnitude of the revisions does not change systematically over the years (i.e., if there is no upward or downward trend in the revisions, such that they are best described by a constant), long-term changes computed from the set of provisional

Comparison of Trend and Cyclical Errors

It is important to distinguish between the characteristics of the errors of the first estimates of long-term movements, or trends, and the errors of the shorter term cyclical changes. The foregoing discussion of trend errors is based on the assumption that the initial estimates of levels are raised in each of the n successive revisions and this is generally true. The exceptions are for levels in the vicinity of cyclical peaks.[52] These estimates have been lowered by the revisions, except for the 1957 peak. If the revisions merely raised the level of the estimates, increases in GNP would be understated and decreases overstated. As we have seen, cyclical (peak to trough) decreases are overstated, but two of the three cyclical (trough to peak) increases are overstated also.

There appears then to have been a systematic difference between cyclical errors and long-term trend errors in the provisional estimates of GNP. The cyclical errors reflect primarily the overestimation of the rise and fall in inventory investment, while the trend errors in the aggregate are dominated by the underestimation errors in personal consumption expenditures.

The two types of error cause the early figures to overestimate cyclical changes and underestimate the trend in GNP. In periods of business cycle contraction, the two kinds of error reinforce each other and cause the initial estimates to exaggerate substantially the severity of peak to trough decline. The errors tend to offset each other during periods of expansion. From 1947 to 1963, the quarters of expansion have greatly outnumbered the quarters of business cycle contraction. Thus an average over the period of the first estimates of quarter-to-quarter changes in GNP would differ little from an average of the revised estimates. This has apparently created the widespread, but mistaken, belief that the revisions have merely raised the level of GNP estimates and have had little systematic effect on the movements.

[52] There are some others; for example, in 1947, 1952, and late 1962. It is tempting to conjecture that these may be associated with periods of retardation and therefore somewhat similar to periods of business cycle contraction.

VII

Summary

The preceding review of the characteristics of GNP revisions is only in a limited sense a study of errors in estimating GNP. First, errors created by conceptual, definitional, and coverage limitations were neglected. Recent work by the Ruggles [53] suggests the magnitude of such errors could be quite large and roughly five to seven times the average size of GNP revisions. Second, the revisions may be only a small component of the errors in measuring GNP, given the particular definitions and scope of the constructs in the present accounts. The crude estimates given in Chapter V suggest the revisions could vary from 8 to 15 per cent of the initial measurement error.

Initial figures for a given quarter are typically revised one month after their publication and again approximately one, two, and three years later as additional data continue to come in. The estimates are further subject to one or more major benchmark revisions such as the one which occurred in August 1965.

The revisions provide an example of one type of measurement error—that resulting from lags in the availability of primary data. The study's emphasis on this one type of error in one set of statistics inherently risks obscuring an important fact: frequent revisions of a given body of data are by no means an indication that it is less reliable than a series that is rarely or never revised. Even though the revisions permit a parade of the inadequacies of the provisional estimates, it would be unwarranted and foolhardy to conclude that these estimates are without value or that they are necessarily less dependable than other series of comparable scope. Indeed, the frequent revisions of GNP estimates should serve as

---

[53] Ruggles, *The Design of Economic Accounts.*

steady reminders that nearly *all* economic statistics contain measurement errors.

Estimates of GNP are built up from detailed component estimates. The comprehensive data underlying many of the components are available only at infrequent intervals and long after the fact. These data are used to construct benchmark estimates. To provide continuous up-to-date series, the movements of a related series are used to interpolate the benchmarks between and to extrapolate them beyond benchmark years. There are then four major sources of error in the provisional estimates: (1) errors in the benchmark estimates; (2) measurement errors in the related series; (3) errors arising from an inexact or misspecified relation between the two variables; and (4) errors arising from extrapolations of past benchmark values.

The revisions were shown to be primarily a measure of the extrapolation errors. The largest revisions were found to be in the GNP components which show considerable variability and weak serial correlation and which would therefore be the most difficult to extrapolate accurately.

The provisional estimates, then, can be viewed as predictions, based on partial information of the values of GNP and its components, and the analysis of their accuracy emphasized their resemblance to forecasts. The questions considered were: the size of the error relative to other forecast and extrapolation errors, how rapidly it is reduced, and whether the accuracy of the estimates has improved over the years. A summary of the findings follows.

Accuracy of the Provisional Estimates

Although they share many of the shortcomings, the provisional GNP estimates for a year just ended are substantially more accurate than business forecasts of GNP for a year ahead. This is true both of total GNP and its major components for the 1953–62 period. The provisional figures are, however, not much more accurate than an average of forecasters' estimates of current annual levels—even though the forecasters publish their estimates some three to four months earlier than the official data.

The forecasts used in these comparisons are from Zarnowitz' sample of several hundred business forecasts which were collected for the NBER short-term forecasting study. Both the forecasts in this sample and the official figures tend to underestimate annual levels of GNP and three of the four major sectors (total consumption, gross private domestic investment, and net exports). Levels of the fourth sector, government expenditures on goods and services, were overestimated on the average.

In addition to comparisons with business forecasts, the accuracy of the provisional estimates of quarterly levels and changes was compared with that of mechanical extrapolations for the 1947–61 period. The provisional figures for levels of aggregates such as GNP, personal consumption expenditures, and gross private domestic investment are considerably more accurate than simple projections, but some of the detailed components do not pass this minimal requirement. For example, initial estimate of the levels of quarterly expenditures of consumer nondurables, producers' durable equipment, new construction, net exports, and of federal government expenditures on goods and services are only about as accurate, and in some cases less accurate, than simple projections.

For many purposes, however, changes are more important than levels. The initial figures for quarterly changes in aggregates, as well as in detailed components, are much more accurate relative to projections than are the initial data for levels. They were, on the average, 40 per cent more accurate than simple projections of "no change" and 10 per cent more accurate than more sophisticated extrapolations.

Success of Revisions and Gains in Accuracy

The sequence of revisions, to be judged successful, should make each set of revised estimates more accurate predictions of the final (1965) figures than are the preceding sets, and as a rule they do. This was shown both in terms of the number of revisions that reduce error and in terms of the magnitude of error reduced.

Successive revisions of the estimates of quarterly change were classified according to whether the revision increased or decreased the previous error. In other words, they were classified according to whether the revision brought the estimate closer to the 1965 figures. Although not all of the revisions were successful, the majority were. About 60 per cent of all of the revisions of all of the components reduced error.

Least successful were the revisions of the advance estimates which occur after only one month. Only about 50 per cent of these revisions reduced error, suggesting that they may not be worth making. It appears that there would be but a small sacrifice in accuracy if revisions of the advance estimates were not made until the first annual July revisions.

In terms of the magnitude of error reduced, major benchmark revisions are clearly the most important. About 60 per cent of the error arising from incomplete primary data remains in the figures until a benchmark revision occurs. Prior to the benchmark revisions, about 25 to 30 per cent of the initial error is eliminated by the revisions occurring approximately two years after the initial figures are published.

Errors in the provisional estimates of quarterly changes in GNP and its components throughout the 1955–61 period were considerably smaller than they were during 1947–54. Extrapolations, however, showed a similar reduction in error. When the reduction in extrapolation error is used as a yardstick, not quite half of the series show greater gains in accuracy. Of these, the greatest improvements were in estimates of producers' durable equipment, change in business inventories, and net exports of goods and services.

Bias in the Initial Estimates of Change in GNP

Although the provisional estimates of quarterly GNP levels show smaller over-all errors than do simple projections throughout the postwar period, a larger proportion of their error consists of bias. Bias, in this context, means a persistent tendency to overestimate, or to underestimate. It is well known that the early figures underestimate levels on the average. Less widely recognized is an element of bias in the initial estimates of quarterly changes. They tend to understate increases and overstate decreases.

In addition, there is a suggestion of bias in the estimates of longer term changes. The initial figures have tended to overestimate cyclical and underestimate trend movements in GNP throughout the postwar period. The cyclical errors were primarily the result of overestimating changes in inventory investment while underestimating changes in personal consumption expenditures was the main source of the trend errors.

During periods of business cycle contraction, the two kinds of error reinforce each other and cause the initial estimates to exaggerate substantially the severity of peak to trough decline in GNP. The errors tend to offset each other during periods of expansion. Throughout the postwar period the quarters of expansion have greatly outnumbered the quarters of business cycle contraction. Thus an average of the first estimates of quarter-to-quarter change in GNP throughout the period would differ little from the average quarterly change in the revised estimates. This has apparently created the widespread, but mistaken, belief that the bias in the initial GNP figures is primarily one of levels and that there are no systematic errors in the early estimates of change.

Expenditures Compared with Income Estimates of GNP

Revisions of the estimates of GNP based on both expenditures and income data were reviewed in order to determine which set yields the more reliable early figures. Occasionally, it is suggested that, despite their shortcomings, the early income figures may be more accurate.

The estimates of GNP based on income are revised less than the expenditures estimates. However, the early income estimates gave only slightly more accurate predictions of the final (i.e., 1965) expenditures figures than the corresponding set of early expenditures estimates. Differences in the primary data which would favor the accuracy of the early income estimates are apparently offset by the lack of early data on profits.

The initial income estimates gave a slightly more accurate indication of the magnitude of decline in GNP during the 1953–54 and 1957–58 contractions than the initial expenditures estimates. The two estimates differ considerably on the amount of decline during 1960–61: the income figures revised in 1965 show a 5.2 billion dollar decrease while the product estimates show a drop of only 1.4 billion in current dollar GNP. Initially they both indicated a decline of about 5.5 billion.

Both estimates have generally agreed on the dates of major turns in GNP, except for the trough in 1954. The expenditures data as revised in 1965 show a trough occurring in the second quarter of 1954 while the income estimates show one in the fourth quarter of 1953. The date of this trough in the product figures has been revised by as much as three quarters (from IV 1953 to III 1954); it was changed only one quarter (IV 1953 to I 1954) in the income estimates.

There has been much less revision in the dates of other major turns. The initial product figures showed the 1949 low point one quarter too early; the income estimates showed the 1960 peak one quarter too late. Until the major revision of 1965 both estimates showed a trough in the first quarter of 1961. The low point now appears in the fourth quarter of 1960.

Consequences for Users of Preliminary Data

The initial figures overestimated the decline in GNP during each of the four postwar contractions. The strength of the increase during the first year of the following expansion was understated in 1950 and in 1954–55, estimated correctly in 1958–59, and overstated in 1961 by the early figures. Thus, throughout the postwar period, economists using movements in GNP as an indicator of the severity of cyclical contractions and of the strength of the following recoveries could have been misled by the figures available at the time.

In addition to underlying analyses of current business conditions, the preliminary data serve as a basis for forecasts. Although there is a wide variety of forecasting techniques, a common thread runs among them. Nearly all forecasts are evaluations of current conditions projected into the future by means of historically observed relationships, whether derived on a formal basis (as in econometric models) or an informal one. Shortcomings in the underlying data are thus transferred to the forecasts.

Though a detailed analysis of the effect of using preliminary rather than revised (1965) GNP data on forecasting accuracy has been made elsewhere, one of the principal findings bears repeating.[54] The use of preliminary data impaired the accuracy of the forecasts examined by a substantial amount: accuracy of naive models was reduced by nearly 30 per cent, while that of business forecasts from the Zarnowitz sample is estimated to have been reduced by an average of about 40 per cent.

[54] R. Cole, "Data Errors and Forecasting Accuracy," in Mincer, ed., *Economic Forecasts and Expectations*.

APPENDIX

An Error Model

A simple error model is developed here in order to illustrate the types of error that GNP estimates may contain and some of the properties of the errors. First considered is the nature of the errors that would be associated with the use of a related series to interpolate between two benchmark estimates; next, the errors that are introduced when the related series consists of preliminary data and is used to extrapolate the last benchmark; and finally, the change in errors when a new benchmark is introduced.

Let ψ denote a variable whose value is known only in benchmark periods 0 and N; and χ, a related variable for which there is a continuous series. Suppose an estimate of the value of ψ in each of the periods between 0 and N is obtained by first interpolating arithmetically and then using deviations in χ from its simple arithmetic trend to estimate the corresponding deviations in ψ.[1] More specifically, suppose that the trend values of ψ and χ in period i, denoted ψ_i^T and χ_i^T, respectively, are estimated as

(1) $\quad \psi_i^T = \psi_0 + \dfrac{i}{N}(\psi_N - \psi_0) \quad$ and

$$\chi_i^T = \chi_0 + \dfrac{i}{N}(\chi_N - \chi_0), \, i = 0, \cdots, N.$$

---

[1] This procedure, which is the one considered by Friedman ("The Interpolation of Times Series"), may or may not be the one actually followed. The specific method used to interpolate and extrapolate the benchmarks is described only as "by means of related series" in the detailed descriptions of how GNP estimates are constructed (*National Income* and *U.S. Income and Output*). However, it is sufficient for the present purpose, which is to illustrate the types of error that the estimates may contain, rather than to estimate the magnitude of the errors or to replicate GNP estimates. Other methods, as Friedman has shown, can be reduced to special cases of his more general one.

If the deviations from these trend values are defined,

(2) $$u_i = \psi_i - \psi_i^T \quad \text{and} \quad v_i = \chi_i - \chi_i^T,$$

and if the unknown u_i were estimated from the known v_i as in

(3) $$u_i = bv_i,$$

then $\hat{\psi}_i$, the estimated value of ψ in period i, would equal

(4) $$\hat{\psi}_i = \psi_i^T + bv_i.$$

If the true relation between u_i and v_i were not an exact one as in (3), but equal instead to

(3') $$u_i = \beta v_i + w_i,$$

then the error in estimating ψ_i would equal

(5) $$\hat{\psi}_i - \psi_i = (b - \beta)v_i - w_i.$$

Thus according to (5), the error in $\hat{\psi}_i$ would consist of the error that would arise if the relation between the movements in the two variables were incorrectly estimated (i.e., if $b \neq \beta$) and because the relation is inexact ($w \neq 0$).

Suppose we now assume that the true values, ψ_0, ψ_N, and χ_i are unknown, but that they are estimated as

(6) $Y_k = \psi_k + \xi_k$ and $X_i = \chi_i + \eta_i$ for $k = 0, N, \cdots$ and $i = 0, \cdots, N, \ldots$, where ξ_k denotes the error in the benchmark estimates (Y_k), and η_i, the measurement error in the related series (X_i). Using these data, the estimate of ψ_i would then become

(7) $$Y_i = \left[Y_0 + \frac{i}{N}(Y_N - Y_0)\right] + b\left[X_i - X_0 - \frac{i}{N}(X_N - X_0)\right]$$

and the error, defined as $E_i = Y_i - \psi_i$, would equal

(8) $$E_i = \left[\xi_0 + \frac{i}{N}(\xi_N - \xi_0)\right] + b\left[\eta_i - \eta_0 - \frac{i}{N}(\eta_N - \eta_0)\right]$$
$$+ [(b - \beta)v_i - w_i].$$

The error in estimating ψ_i would thus consist of errors in the benchmark estimates (ξ), measurement errors in the related variable (η), and errors due to an inexact or incorrectly estimated relationship between the movements in the two variables.

Appendix

Let ξ_k and η_i be stationary to the second order with means μ_ξ and μ_η and variances $\sigma^2(\xi)$ and $\sigma^2(\eta)$. The expected value (denoted E) of E_i would then equal

(9) $\quad E(E_i) = \mu_\xi$, provided that $E(v_i)$ and $E(w_i)$ are zero for all i.

As (9) shows, Y_i would be a biased estimate of ψ_i unless μ_ξ equals zero. But even if $\mu_\xi \neq 0$, it is readily shown that the implicit estimate of the change in ψ from period i to period $i+1$ would be unbiased. Since Y_{i+1} would equal

$$Y_{i+1} = \left[Y_0 + \frac{i+1}{N}(Y_N - Y_0)\right] + b\left[X_{i+1} - X_0 - \frac{i+1}{N}(X_N - X_0)\right],$$

the implicit estimate of change would equal

(10) $\quad \Delta Y_{i+1} = \frac{1}{N}(Y_N - Y_0) + b\left[X_{i+1} - X_i - \frac{1}{N}(X_N - X_0)\right],$

and the error would equal

(11) $\quad E_{\Delta i+1} = \frac{1}{N}(\xi_N - \xi_0) + b\left[\eta_{i+1} - \eta_i - \frac{1}{N}(\eta_N - \eta_0)\right]$
$\quad\quad\quad\quad\quad + [(b - \beta)(v_{i+1} - v_i) - (w_{i+1} - w_i)].$

On the previous assumption of stationarity, the expected value of $E_{\Delta i+1}$ is

(12) $\quad E(E_{\Delta i+1}) = 0$, provided $E(v)$ and $E(w)$ are zero for all i.

The change estimates would therefore be unbiased even if the level estimates were not.

It might be tempting to conclude that this result supports the widespread notion that estimates of changes (say, in GNP) are more reliable than estimates of levels. However, this is not necessarily true. The accuracy of change estimates relative to that of levels depends on the relative importance of the error components and bias is only one element of over-all error. If, for example, benchmark errors were by far the most important source of error, then the mean square error levels would exceed the mean square error of changes. On the other hand, if the relation between the movements in ψ and χ were not strong and if it were incorrectly estimated, then benchmark errors (and errors in measuring χ) could be relatively minor components of the error in estimating levels and changes in ψ. In this case, the mean square error of changes could exceed that of levels.[2]

Errors in Provisional Estimates

Thus far we have considered the errors in estimating ψ when movements in a related series X are used to interpolate between two known benchmarks, Y_0 and Y_N. These, however, are the errors that could be expected in "final" or benchmark revised estimates rather than in the estimates that are published on a current basis. Provisional estimates of the current value of ψ in each of the periods between 0 and N must be made without benefit of Y_N. Such estimates are essentially extrapolations rather than interpolations, and their errors will differ accordingly.

To illustrate, suppose that a provisional estimate, made in period i, of the value of ψ_i were constructed by first extrapolating the last known benchmark period estimate and then using the deviation in the related series from its extrapolated trend to estimate the corresponding deviation in ψ_i.[3] In addition, suppose that only preliminary estimates of χ, denoted X°, are available at the time the provisional estimates of ψ are prepared. The provisional estimate, Y_i°, would then be

$$(13) \quad Y_i^\circ = \left[Y_0 + \frac{i}{N}(\psi_N^* - Y_0) \right] + b\left[X_i^\circ - X_0 - \frac{i}{N}(\chi_N^* - X_0) \right],$$

where ψ_N^* and χ_N^* denote predictions of ψ_N and χ_N, respectively. If the prediction errors and the errors in the preliminary estimates of χ are defined as

$$\epsilon(\psi)_N = \psi_N^* - \psi_N; \quad \epsilon(\chi)_N = \chi_N^* - \chi_N; \quad \text{and } \eta^\circ = X_i^\circ - \chi_i,$$

the error in the provisional estimate, defined as $E_i^\circ = Y_i^\circ - \psi_i$, would equal

$$E_i^\circ = \left[\xi_0 + \frac{i}{N}(\epsilon(\psi)_N - \xi_0) \right] + b\left[\eta_i^\circ - \eta_0 - \frac{i}{N}(\epsilon(\chi)_N - \eta_0) \right]$$
$$+ (b - \beta)v_i - w_i.$$

[2] If ξ and η were relatively unimportant, the mean square errors would be

$$M(E_i) \approx (b - \beta)^2 \sigma^2(v_i) + \sigma^2(w_i)$$
$$M(E_{\Delta i}) \approx (b - \beta)^2 \sigma^2(v_{i+1} - v_i) + \sigma^2(w_{i+1} - w_i).$$

Unless there is strong positive serial correlation in v or in w,

$$M(E_{\Delta i}) > M(E_i).$$

[3] See footnote 1 on p. 97.

Using (8), E_i° can also be expressed as

(13) $\quad E_i^\circ = E_i + \dfrac{i}{N}\left[\epsilon(\psi)_N - \xi_N) - b(\epsilon(\chi)_N - \eta_N)\right] + b(\eta_i^\circ - \eta_i).$

With the aid of (13), the differences in accuracy between the provisional and the revised estimates of ψ become fully visible. The error in the provisional estimate (E_i°) would exceed the error in the revised estimate (E_i as long as: (1) the errors in the predictions, made in period i, of the values of ψ_N and χ_N exceed the error in the benchmark estimate, Y_N, and the measurement error in X_N (i.e., if $\epsilon(\psi)_N$ and $\epsilon(\chi)_N$ exceed ξ_N and η_N, respectively) and; (2) the error in the estimate based on preliminary data exceeds the error in the revised estimate of χ_i (i.e., $\eta_i^\circ > \eta_i$).

It is often contended that merely the fact that national accounts estimates are revised offers no guarantee that the revised estimates are more accurate than the initial figures. We have seen, however, that within the framework of the present model, the major revisions could be viewed as replacing predictions, made before period N occurs, with estimates, based on data from period N, of ψ_N and χ_N. In order for the revised estimates to be only as accurate as the initial figures, the predictions, ψ_N^* and χ_N^*, would have to be as accurate as the later estimates, Y_N and X_N. Since the predictions would rely to some extent on the last known benchmark estimate, Y_0, and on preliminary estimates of χ (X°), any errors in these data would be transmitted to the predictions and become a component of their errors. Thus in the absence of evidence that the accuracy of the benchmark estimates and data for the related series has deteriorated over time (such that Y_0 and X° are more accurate than Y_N and X), it is reasonable to suppose that predictions would be less accurate than estimates of ψ_N and χ_N and hence to reject the contention that the revised estimates are no more accurate (let alone *less* accurate) than the provisional estimates

Errors Measured by the Revisions

The revisions are defined as the difference between provisional and revised estimates. Both Y_i° and Y_i can be expressed as

$$Y_i^\circ = \psi_i + E_i^\circ \quad \text{and} \quad Y_i = \psi_i + E_i,$$

the sum of the true value and the respective errors of estimate. The revision would then equal

$$Y_i^\circ - Y_i = E_i^\circ - E_i,$$

which, using (13), can be expressed

(14) $$Y_i^\circ - Y_i = \frac{i}{N}[\epsilon(Y)_N - b\epsilon(X)_N] + b\epsilon_i,$$

where $\epsilon(Y)_N = \epsilon(\psi)_N - \xi_N$; $\epsilon(X)_N = \epsilon(x)_N - \eta_N$; and $\epsilon_i = \eta_i^\circ - \eta_i$. Since $\epsilon(Y)_N$ and $\epsilon(X)_N$ would also equal $\psi_N^* - Y_N$ and $x_N^* - x_N$, respectively,[4] the revisions would be a measure of the errors in predicting Y_N and X_N and of the reduction in measurement errors in the preliminary data on χ. The prediction errors $\epsilon(Y)$ and $\epsilon(X)$ would be a common component of the revision in the provisional estimates of ψ in each period between 0 and N, and thus a source of positive serial correlation in the revisions. Moreover, the importance of the prediction error would increase with i and hence the revisions would grow larger as i increases.

It is readily shown that the revisions in estimates of period-to-period changes would not depend on i and that they would be smaller than the revisions in level estimates, provided prediction errors were a major component of the revisions. Since

$$Y_{i+1}^\circ - Y_i = \frac{i+1}{N}[\epsilon(Y)_N - b\epsilon(X)_N] + b\epsilon_{i+1},$$

the revision in ΔY_{i+1}° would equal

(15) $$\Delta Y_{i+1}^\circ - \Delta Y_{i+1} = \frac{1}{N}[\epsilon(Y)_N - b\epsilon(X)_N] + b(\epsilon_{i+1} - \epsilon_i).$$

Let both the predictions and the preliminary data be unbiased. The mean square revision of the level would then be

(16) $$M = \left[\frac{i+1}{N}\right]^2 \sigma^2(\epsilon(Y)_N - b\epsilon(X)_N) + b^2\sigma^2(\epsilon),$$

and of the change,

(17) $$M_\Delta = \frac{1}{N^2}\sigma^2(\epsilon(Y)_N - b\epsilon(X)_N) + 2b^2\sigma^2(\epsilon),$$

provided $\mathrm{Cov}(\epsilon, \epsilon(Y)_N - b\epsilon(X)_N)$ and $\mathrm{Cov}(\epsilon_{i+1}, \epsilon_i)$ are zero. Thus M would exceed M_Δ if the prediction errors were the major component, and more specifically if $\sigma^2(\epsilon(Y)_N - b\epsilon(X)_N) > \dfrac{2N^2}{i(i+2)}b^2\sigma^2(\epsilon)$.

---

[4] This is seen by writing

$$\epsilon(Y)_N = \epsilon(\psi)_N - \xi_N = \epsilon(\psi_N^* - \psi_N) - (Y_N - \psi_N) = \psi_N^* - Y_N$$

and

$$\epsilon(X)_N = \epsilon(x)_N - \eta_N = (x_N^* - x_N) - (X_N - x_N) = x_N^* - X_N.$$

Finally, if the predictions were extrapolations of the last known benchmark period estimates, the variance of their errors would be

(18) $\sigma^2[\epsilon(Y)] = (1 - \rho_Y^2)\sigma^2(Y)$ and $\sigma^2[\epsilon(X)] = (1 - \rho_X^2)\sigma^2(X)$,

where ρ_Y and ρ_X are the coefficients of serial correlation. In this case then, the magnitude of the errors would depend on the variability and the strength of the serial correlation in the series to be predicted.

Index

Anticipation series, 28
Auto and appliance maintenance and repairs, 10–11

Balance of payments, net exports data and, 13
Benchmark estimates
 errors in, 14, 18
 revisions of, 49
Bias in estimates of changes in GNP, 94–95
Biennial Survey of Education, 11
Budget of the U.S. government, 13
Building permits, new construction estimates and, 11
Bureau of the Census, *see* U.S. Bureau of the Census
Bureau of Labor Statistics, *see* U.S. Bureau of Labor Statistics
Business cycles, 23
 and GNP estimates, 6, 69t, 70, 71t, 72t, 73, 74t–79t, 80–81
 bias in, 94–95
 errors in, 6, 22–23, 23t, 26, 91–92
 and postwar trends, 84–90
 and seasonal factors, 81
Business and Defense Administration, 11–12
Business fixed investment, construction components of, 11
Business forecasts of GNP
 accuracy of, 92–93
 compared with provisional estimates, 29, 30t, 31t, 32t, 32–33, 34t, 35, 92–93
 error statistics for, 22t
 errors in, 36t
  overestimation and underestimation and, 26

 and forecasts of seasonal patterns, 84
Business inventories estimates
 errors in, 25t
 compared with naive model projection errors, 43t
 and gains over time, 58t
 and successive revisions, 50t, 52t
 and GNP estimates, 12–13
 and seasonal patterns of GNP, 82, 83t, 84

Census Bureau, *see* U.S. Bureau of the Census
Cloos, George W., 80n
Cole, Rosanne, 26n, 96n
Commodities, benchmark estimates for, 8–10
Commodity flow estimates, 8–9
 of producers' durables, 12
Construction, *see* New construction; Public utility construction; Nonfarm residential construction
Consumer durables estimates
 errors in, 24t
 compared with errors in naive model projections, 41t
 and gains over time, 57t
 and successive revisions, 53t
Consumer goods expenditures, *see* Personal consumption expenditures
Consumer nondurables estimates
 errors in, 24t
 compared with errors in naive model projections, 42t
 and gains over time, 57t
 and successive revisions, 53t
Consumer services estimates
 errors in, 24t
 compared with errors in naive model projections, 42t

and successive revisions, 53t
See also Personal consumption expenditures
Contract awards, construction estimates and, 11
Contractions, *see* Business cycles
Council of Economic Advisers, 16, 29n
Cyclical changes, *see* Business cycles
Cyclical errors, *see* Business cycles and gross national product estimates

Deane, Phyllis, 4n
Definitional changes in GNP, 35n
DeJanosi, Peter E., 4n
Direction-of-change errors, 23, 24t, 25t, 25–27
Dodge series, 11
Domestic investment, *see* Gross private domestic investment
Domestic service expenditure estimates, 10
Durables, *see* Consumer durables
Dutch GNP forecasts, 48

Economic Indicators, 16
Economic Report of the President, 16, 29n, 32n
Employment data, 11
Error model, 18, 97
Error statistics
 for business forecasts of GNP, 22t
 for estimates of GNP, 20t
  compared with forecasts, 29, 30t, 31t, 32t, 32–33, 34t, 35
 and successive revisions of GNP estimates and forecasts, 48–56
 See also Errors in GNP estimates
Errors in GNP estimates
 and business cycles, 94–95
 calculation methods, 100–103
 compared with errors in forecasts and naive model projections, 36t, 41t
 and errors in expenditures and income estimates, 62, 63t, 63–64
 and gains over time, 56–61
 trend and cyclical, 90–92
 and use of preliminary data, 96
 use of statistical discrepancy to measure, 64–68

See also Error statistics; Gross national product estimates, errors in
Expenditures estimates
 errors in, 62, 63t, 63–64
 and GNP estimates, 95–96
 See also Government expenditures; Personal consumption expenditures
Exports, net, *see* Net exports of goods and services
Extrapolation errors, 15n
 and errors in early GNP data, 56
 and errors in GNP estimates, 17–22
 and GNP revisions, 28, 62, 64–68

Farm inventory estimates, 13
Farm and public utility construction data, 11
Federal Aviation Administration, 10
Federal Reserve Board
 Index of Industrial Production, 80
 Survey of Consumer Finances, 11
Final expenditures estimates, 63t
Final purchases, season pattern of GNP and, 83t, 84
Forecaster, task of, 29
Forecasts of GNP, *see* Business forecasts of GNP
Friedman, Milton, 14n, 97n
F. W. Dodge Corporation, 11

GNP, *see* Gross national product; Business forecasts of GNP; Gross national product estimates; Gross national product extrapolations
Goldberg, Simon, 4n
Goods and services, *see* Government expenditures on goods and services; Net exports of goods and services
Government expenditures on goods and services
 error statistics for estimates of, 20t
 error statistics for forecasts of, 22t
 errors in estimates of, 25t
 and cyclical characteristics of quarter covered, 23t
 and gains over time, 58t

Government expenditures on goods and services, errors in estimates of (cont.)
  and successive revisions, 48, 50*t*, 52*t*, 54*t*, 89*t*
  errors in forecasts and estimates compared, 31*t*, 36*t*
  errors in naive model projections and estimates compared, 36*t*, 44*t*
  and GNP estimates, 13–14
  overestimates of, 32
Gross national product (GNP)
  average rates of change of, 86–87, 88
  decline in, 68–81
  exclusive of statistical discrepancy, 87*t*
  peak to trough changes in components of, 72*t*, 74*t*
  postwar trends in, 84–90
  seasonal pattern of, 82, 83*t*, 84
  See also Business forecasts of GNP; Gross national product estimates
Gross national product estimates
  accuracy of, 4–5, 92–93
  based on expenditures and income data, 64–68
  bias in, 94–95
  and business cycles, 69*t*, 70, 71*t*, 72*t*, 73, 74*t*–79*t*, 80–81
  and change in business inventories, 12–13
  of changes and levels compared, 99–100
  compared with extrapolations, 35–47
  compared with GNP forecasts, 29, 30*t*, 31*t*, 32–33, 34*t*, 35, 92–93
  and comparison of trend and cyclical errors, 90–92
  construction of, 97*n*
  data and methods used in, 8–14
  data sources, 7–8
  and definitional changes, 17
  error statistics for, 20*t*
  errors in, 38*t*–39*t*, 41*t*–45*t*
    characteristics of, 18
    compared with errors in naive model projections, 41*t*
    created by limitations of concepts, definitions, and coverage, 3
    cyclical characteristics of, 22–23, 23*t*
    and errors in expenditures and income estimates, 62, 63*t*, 63–64
    major sources of, 14
    measurement of, 64–68, 100–103
    overestimation, underestimation, and direction-of-change errors, 23, 24*t*, 25*t*, 25–27
    resemblance to extrapolation errors, 17–22
    revised estimates as measure of, 4–5
    types of, potential of revisions and, 14–17
  establishment of, 7
  evaluation of, 91–92
  and federal government purchases of goods and services, 13
  first, 16, 87*t*
  and gains over time, 56–61
  and gains through successive revisions, 48–56
  and incorporation of new benchmarks, 16–17
  and major patterns of change, 6
  major revisions in, 17
  minor revisions in, 15
  and net exports of goods and services, 13
  and new construction, 11–12
  peak to trough decline in, 6
  and personal consumption expenditures, 9–11
  and producer's durable equipment expenditures, 12
  and revisions of seasonal factors, 81–82, 83*t*, 84
  and state and local purchases of goods and services, 13–14
  and successive revisions, 93–94
  turning-point dates in, 78*t*–79*t*
  and use of expenditures and income data compared, 95–96
  and use of preliminary data, 96–100
  uses of, 3
Gross national product extrapolations compared with provisional estimates, 35–47

Index

Gross national product forecasts, *see* Business forecasts of GNP
Gross private domestic investment
  error statistics for average business forecasts of, 22*t*
  error statistics for estimates of, 20*t*
  errors in estimates of, 24*t*
    compared with forecast errors and naive model projection errors, 31*t*, 36*t*, 42*t*
    and cyclical characteristics of quarter covered, 23*t*
    and gains over time, 57*t*
    and successive revisions, 50*t*, 52*t*
  first estimates compared with revised average annual rates of increase in, 89*t*
  long-term changes in, 88–89
  successive revisions in estimates of, 53*t*

Home rental value estimates, 10
Household utilities expenditure estimates, 10
Housing statistics, 11–12

Income estimates
  compared with consumption estimates, 10*n*
  errors in, 62, 63*t*, 63–64
  and gross national product estimates, 95–96
  as predictions of final expenditures, 63*t*
  and product estimates, 7–8
Input-output data, 17
Interest paid by consumers, 17*n*
Internal Revenue Service tax return data, 12–13
Interstate Commerce Commission, 10
Investment, *see* Gross private domestic investment

Jaszi, George, 4, 4*n*

Kuznets, Simon, 8

Laundry expenditures estimates, 10–11
LIFO inventories, 13

Magnitudes of business cycles, 69–70
Maintenance and repairs, *see* Auto and appliance maintenance and repairs
Mean square errors
  in forecasts of GNP, 29
  in GNP estimates, business cycles and, 23*t*
  in naive projections of GNP, 34*t*
  See also Error statistics; Errors in GNP estimates
Mincer, Jacob, 26*n*
Moore, Geoffrey H., 40*t*, 81
Morgenstern, Oskar, 4*n*

Naive model projections errors, 34*t*, 36*t*
Nassimbene, Raymond, 4
National Housing Inventory, 12
National income estimates, 14*n*
Net exports of goods and services estimates, 13, 32*n*–33*n*, 52*t*
  error statistics for, 20*t*
  errors in, 25*t*
    compared with forecast errors, 32*t*
    compared with forecast and naive model projection errors, 37*t*
    compared with naive model projection errors, 45*t*
    and cyclical characteristics of quarter covered, 23*t*
    and gains over time, 58*t*
    and successive revisions, 50*t*, 54*t*
Net exports of goods and services business forecasts, 32*t*
  error statistics for, 22*t*
New construction estimates
  errors in, 24*t*
    compared with naive model projection errors, 43*t*
    and gains over time, 57*t*
    and successive revisions, 50*t*, 52*t*
  and GNP estimates, 11–12
  successive revisions of, 54*t*
Noncorporate sector business inventories data, 12
Nonfarm residential construction, 11

Overestimation, 86–87
  of GNP components, 88–90
  of GNP decline, 70, 73

Overestimation (cont.)
  in GNP estimates, 23, 24t, 25t, 25–27
  and use of preliminary GNP data, 96–100
OBE, see U.S. Department of Commerce, Office of Business Economics
Oil and gas well drilling estimates, 11

Passenger car expenditures, 12
Payroll data, 11
  and government purchases estimates, 14
Peak to trough changes in GNP, 71t, 74t–77t
Personal consumption expenditures estimates
  error statistics for, 20t
  errors in, 24t
    compared with errors in forecasts of, 31t, 36t
    compared with errors in naive model projections of, 36t, 41t
    and cyclical characteristics of quarter covered, 23t
    and gains over time, 57t
    and GNP trend errors, 6
    and successive revisions, 50t, 52t
    first estimate compared with revised average annual rates of, 89t
    and GNP estimates, 9–11
  underestimation of, 2–3
Personal consumption expenditures, 22t
Plant and equipment outlays estimates, 15
Policy-makers, GNP estimates and, 80–81
Prediction error, 18
Preliminary data in GNP estimates, 96–100
Private domestic investment, see Gross private domestic investment
Producers' durable equipment estimates, 94
  errors in, 24t
    compared with errors in naive model projections of, 43t
    and gains over time, 57t

  and successive revisions, 50t, 52t, 53t
  and GNP estimates, 12
Product estimates compared with income estimates, 7–8
Product flows, 16n
Production, interest and, 17n
Professional services expenditures estimates, 10
Public utility construction estimates, 11

Recoveries, see Business cycles
Recreation expenditures, 10–11
Retail sales estimates
  and consumption expenditures estimates, 9–10
  revisions in, 15
"Revision errors," 5
Revisions, successive, 48–56, 93–94
Root mean square errors in GNP estimates, 35, 51
  compared with errors in naive projections, 38t
Ruggles, Nancy, 3n, 8n, 91
Ruggles, Richard, 3n, 8n, 91

Sales, 16n, 17n
Sampling error, 14
Seasonal factors and GNP estimates, 59, 81–82, 83t, 84
Shiskin, Julius, 40t
Spearman coefficients, 19
Statistical discrepancy and error measurement, 64–68
Statistics of Income, 12
Stekler, H. O., 4n, 5, 51n, 56, 80
Survey of Current Business, 16, 32n

Teeter, Benjamin T., 4
Theil, Henri, 48, 51n
Timing adjustments, new construction estimates and, 11
Trade associations, annual reports of, 10
Transportation expenditures estimates, 10
Trend errors, 90–92
Trough to peak changes in GNP, 72t, 73
Turning-point dates in GNP, 73, 78t–79t, 80

Underestimation, 86–87
  of GNP components, 88–90
  in GNP estimates, 23, 24t, 25t, 25–27
U.S. Bureau of the Census
  Annual Survey of Manufactures, 10, 12
  Census of Agriculture, 10
  Census of Business, 11
  census data, GNP revisions and, 16
  Census of Population and Housing, 10
  Census of Manufactures, 9
  Census of Religious Bodies, 11
  Census of Retail Trade, 9–10
  new construction data, 11
  retail sales data, 9
  summary statistics on state and local finances, 13

U.S. Bureau of Labor Statistics, 11
  Consumer Price Index, 11
  Survey of Consumer Expenditures, 11
U.S. Department of Agriculture, 13
U.S. Department of Commerce, Office of Business Economics (OBE), 7, 16, 81–82
U.S. government
  budget, 13
  Monthly Statement of Receipts and Expenditures, 13
U.S. Treasury, 13

Within year patterns of GNP, 59

Zarnowitz, Victor, 21, 26, 27, 32n, 33n, 37n, 80n
Zellner, Arnold, 4n, 35n, 56